Orange Blossom & Honey

John Gregory-Smith is a food and travel journalist who has written three previous books, *Turkish Delights*, *Mighty Spice Express,* and *Mighty Spice Cookbook*. He travels all over the world in search of the best recipes and latest food trends, contributing regularly to various publications such as *GQ, Men's Health,* and the *Daily Mail.* And when not heading off the beaten track, his London pop-ups always receive rave reviews. Catch him on instagram: @johngs

Orange Blossom & Honey

MAGICAL MOROCCAN RECIPES FROM THE SOUKS TO THE SAHARA

JOHN GREGORY-SMITH

Food photography by Martin Poole
Location photography by Alan Keohane

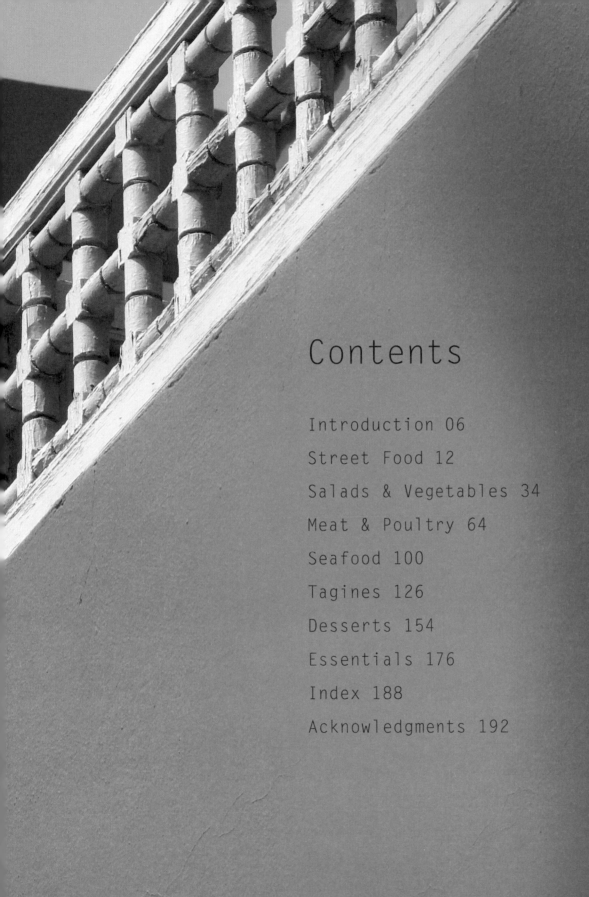

Contents

The Land of the Setting Sun

From as early as the seventh century, the Arabs referred to North Africa as Maghrib—The Land of the Setting Sun. Morocco was the end of their world, and the start of the West. For me, Morocco is not an ending, but a beginning—a gateway to the East, and a world that's so amazing I can't fully describe it; it's the land of the setting sun and of a million stars, of mountain ranges and deserts, of stunning cities and coastal villages. It's the source of a culinary obsession that has lasted many years and will without doubt last many more.

My first trip to Morocco was in 2007 after reading about the ancient medina of Fez. I was fascinated by the stories of winding alleyways, hidden houses, and night markets; I knew I had to go and see it first hand. And after what seemed like ages, leaving London and traveling via Marrakesh to the north of Morocco, I finally arrived in the dead of night.

With the help of the world's smallest torch, a guide led me into the medina—the walled section of the city. As we made our way through the narrow streets, the torch's tiny beam revealed a glimpse of the city's splendor. Stunning doorways, embossed with geometrical patterns, broke up the towering stone walls that surrounded us, and I caught glimpses of ornate gardens hidden behind rickety wooden gates.

The next morning I ate breakfast on the hotel's terrace, looking over a thousand rooftops squeezed so tightly together that you couldn't see the streets beneath them. But I could hear them, bubbling away. A world of spices and souks, a million miles from anything I'd ever seen before, was opening up. I was hooked.

The Feisty Flavors of Morocco

Although the Sahara Desert occupies swathes of the country to the south, Morocco is incredibly fertile. The vast coastal plains and expansive plateaus of the northwest, between the great cities of Rabat and Marrakesh, are rich with crops. Stretching as far as the eye can see, from the blustery Atlantic coast to the mountains in the east, everything from wheat to citrus fruits and an abundance of vegetables, herbs, and pulses is grown.

Meandering down into the waters of the Mediterranean Sea, the Rif Mountains score their way across the north of the country. Subsistence farmers grow herbs, fruits, and cereal crops on lush ledges, high in the mountains. Deep in the desert, natural oases breath life into the land and sticky-sweet dates droop down from palm trees.

All over the country, even in the most remote regions high in the Atlas Mountains, cattle, sheep, goats, and chickens are reared (for religious reasons, pork is not widely eaten). Along the golden coastlines, there's an abundance of fresh fish and other seafood, including Oualidia's famous oysters.

Ginger, paprika, turmeric, and cumin are all produced in Morocco and used in abundance in the country's cooking. To add more character to special dishes, elaborate spice blends like ras el hanout (page 180), chermoula (pages 180, 183) and *baharat*—a musty mix of ground pepper, clove, and cumin—are used. They are bought in the market, ready ground, in small quantities to keep fresh and full of flavor.

The food of this great country is what keeps me coming back, time after time. I'm guessing many of you will have eaten in a Moroccan restaurant or two, and quite possibly had the pleasure of a vacation in Marrakesh. But the real food of Morocco is served at home and eaten with friends and family: delicately steamed couscous that's topped with meat, vegetables, and cinnamon-spiced onions; rich Berber tagines, little *kefta* cooked in thick sauces with egg, savory, fruity salads, sweet stews, and sensational seafood. Everything is seasonal and made with local ingredients. Flavors such as saffron, powdered ginger, cumin, preserved lemons, honey, olives, and orange blossom, elevate the everyday into the extraordinary. And a rich history of different cultures coming and going has added even more color to the food of this already-vibrant land.

Today's Moroccan food is a cultural clash of Berber and Arabic, with other influences peppered in. Exiled Moors from Spain brought olive cultivation, citrus fruits, and paprika, and the Jewish Moors, preserving and pickling. When you visit the Jewish quarter, or *mellah*, in Marrakesh or Fez today, you'll find pickled vegetables and preserved lemons piled high, just waiting for your best offer. The mighty Ottoman Empire introduced a little fire and smoke through their chargrilled kebabs and the French, who had a protectorate on Morocco from 1912 and occupied the country for 40 years, left their café culture and an appetite for sophisticated pastries and breads. Along the Mediterranean coast in the north, the Spanish influence can be seen, and you can feast on Moroccaned-up versions of classic recipes like paella and *boquerónes*.

Culture Clashes & Dynasty Downfalls

The original inhabitants of Morocco were the Berbers, native tribes of North Africa who have lived in the region since around 10,000 BC.

Berber comes from the Greek word *barbaria*, their name for the Maghrib region—"the land of the barbarians." But the Berbers refer to themselves as Amazigh, which can be translated as "free people" or "noble men," and their longevity is testament to this more accurate etymology. They have outlasted any ruling empire and their incredible culture still thrives today, including their language, Tamazigh, which was recently awarded official status alongside Arabic. Outside the big cities you can find traditional agricultural Berber villages, where the language and customs have remained relatively unchanged for thousands of years.

As a whole, Morocco has absorbed aspects of the various cultures that have passed through it over the centuries. Standing between the mighty Sahara Desert and the Mediterranean Sea, it was perfectly positioned as an outpost for different civilizations. From the Byzantines to the Phoenicians, Romans, and later the Arabs, ruling empires passed through, making the most of the fertile land and trusted trade routes.

Arguably, it was the Arabs who were one of the biggest influences on Morocco. In the seventh century they marched from Medina on the Arabian Peninsula, gathering more troops in Egypt, and made their way across to Morocco. There, they introduced their religion and language to the country—and they also left their mark on the cuisine. From the refined royal kitchens of Baghdad, the Arabs imparted a new world of exotic spices, nuts, and dried fruits. They blended sweet with savory and meat with fruit, techniques they had learned from the great kitchens of Persia. With the introduction of Islam came certain practices, like breaking the fast during the month of Ramadan with *harira* soup (page 26), bread and sweet dates, or slaughtering a lamb for the celebration of Eid Al Adha.

The Arab armies joined forces with the Berbers. Together they crossed the narrow Strait of Gibraltar and swept north, invading Spain

(where they had a stronghold for nearly 500 years) and Portugal. These invaders were known as the Moors and the land they commanded was referred to as *al-Andalus*.

From the eleventh century, two great Berber dynasties ruled in Morocco, taking control from the ruling Arab empire—first the Almoravids, from the Sahara, and then the Almohads from Tinmel, deep in the heart of the Atlas Mountains. Marrakesh was their capital. There they built the great Koutoubia Mosque in the twelfth century. The towering turquoise minaret still stands today, dominating the skyline around Jemaa el Fna Square.

The Moors began to lose their hold on Spain from around 1212 AD, first losing the cities of Sevilla and Cordoba. By the seventeenth century, they had been completely expelled from Spain by Philip III. They returned to northern Morocco to continue practicing their Islamic faith rather than converting to Christianity. They brought with them Spanish food and architecture, and at the same time left their own footprint in southern Spain. In fact, my favorite building in Granada, the Alhambra Palace, is a triumph of eleventh-century Moorish architecture.

The Alaouite Dynasty united the warring tribes of Morocco and has been the ruling house of the country since 1666. Although the dynasty did well to establish Morocco as a united country, there were times of instability. In 1912, following the Treaty of Fez, France intervened and established a protectorate in Morocco. Spain was also given zones in northern Morocco and the Western Sahara, areas that remain disputed to this day. In 1956, Morocco gained independence, although Spain retained a coastal foothold until the 1970s. Today, it's clear to see that both countries left their mark on Moroccan culture and cuisine.

Throughout this rich and varied history, the Berbers have remained. Currently there are different Berber tribes across Morocco, including the Drawa Berbers who inhabit the Drâa Valley, the Dades in the Dades Valley, and the Gormara in the Rif Mountains. They are an essential part of the intricate tapestry of this country, and even Moroccans who do not identify as Berber will have a strong Berber cultural heritage.

Food, Friends, & Family

Moroccan food and hospitality is legendary. My first real experience of this was in the High Atlas Mountains, visiting my friend Lachen's village, Tacheddirt. Complete with an inappropriate wheelie suitcase, I was dropped off where the road stopped and the terrain took over; rolling hills and rocky ledges replaced the tarmac, and nestled below was the little village. My host gave up his sturdy donkey for my case, and we walked behind to his home. It had been a long journey from Marrakesh, and they had gone all out to welcome me—the whole family was there with a fabulous chicken tagine, steaming cups of sweet mint tea, freshly baked bread, and colorful chopped salads. I was greeted like an old friend, and we sat outside feasting and watched one of the greatest views in the world. Lunch rolled into tea, which soon became dinner, and new friends drifted in and out of the meals. It was truly wonderful.

Another memorable moment from my travels was meeting Fouad, a truly remarkable character. He owned a restuarant in Chefchaouen, which is perhaps one of my favorite places in Morocco, a small town high in the Rif Mountains, in the north of the country. Known as The Blue Pearl, the old medina is painted different shades of blue. It's so surreal, like being on a movie set, everything from the streets to the pavements and houses, all different hues of blue. The town has a long history, heavy with Andalusian influence, which is seen in the architecture and incredible food. When I arrived at Fouad's tiny restaurant to meet him, it was shut. I waited and, finally, when I was almost about to give up, he ambled up the street and introduced himself to me. A trained chef, he had worked in restaurants all over the country, but had returned to the town to make home-cooked, Spanish-Moroccan food for the locals.

Fouad's restaurant was quite mad. The ancient kitchen was packed with everything from chipped pots and pans to broken cassette players and out of date guidebooks. He started cooking and talking, instinctively knowing his way around the ingredients. Other guests came in and my meal was sidelined as he whipped up a quick plate of *kefta* or sardine tagine. It was all very *Fawlty Towers*, as he clattered and crashed around the restaurant. But his food was subtly spiced and utterly beautiful. I spent several days working with him to learn everything I could. His wood-fired paella is legendary, and he has given me the recipe for my book (page 124). He also showed me how to make his beautiful Chermoula Spiced Chicken (page 79).

An equally amazing experience came about by chance while I was staying with my travel photographer for this book, Alan Keohane. As we arrived in Alan's village, just outside Marrakesh, we met a very glamorous woman, complete with oversized shades and sunhat. She was more Audrey Hepburn than local housewife. She turned out to be Alan's neighbor, Beatriz. When I told her I was researching this book, she invited me to stay in her desert house in Skoura, on the edge of the Oasis in the Drâa Valley. The house is a traditional mud-build, but with chic rustic interiors, a jet-black pool and stunning views of the palm trees and surrounding mountains. Frankly, I couldn't believe my luck.

My hosts were Muhammad and his mother Aicha. They had looked after the house for years, he an English teacher with a cut-glass accent and cheeky glint in his eye, and she a traditional Berber lady with tribal tattoos and vibrant clothing. Despite the language barrier between us, Aicha was so warm and welcoming and cooked me some of the most fantastic food I have ever eaten. Tasting her lamb *medfouna* and drinking thick black coffee in the hazy morning sun, overlooking the oasis was blissful. She took me though a selection of traditional Saharan foods from her village; couscous flecked with fresh chives (Herby Couscous, page 52), pepper-spiked tagines, and on my last day she handed me a whole cow's leg to saw in half and stew with beans (trust me, this was incredible). Some of her dishes are in this book— although the whole cow's leg recipe had to be adapted somewhat! (See *Lubiah Belkarah*, page 94.) In addition to feeding me so well, they also drove me to dusty cattle markets in forgotten villages, to marvel at ancient kasbahs, and cool off in hidden lakes. I saw an undiscovered side of Morocco; rural, calm, and welcoming, and I fell in love with it.

It was experiences such as these which allowed me to enjoy the best of Morocco, exploring off the beaten track, and which led me to write this book. Each adventure, every encounter, is linked by a common love of food and the way it brings people together. It is so integral to the culture of Morocco, and something I want to share.

I am at my happiest writing books; off in the hills learning from the locals, finding new and exciting dishes that capture the essence of a country. I love going through my notes, working up the recipes in my kitchen and putting pen to paper. *Orange Blossom & Honey* is my fourth book, and a window into a wonderful world. From the Sahara to the sea and the mountains to the medinas, I hope these recipes will bring a little Moroccan magic into your kitchen. So let the aromas of spice-scented tagines and freshly cooked breads mingle with the chatter of friends and family around your dining table—*insha'Allah*.

Street Food

Night Stall Noodles
& Ox Cheeks

Serves 4

2 (1-pound) ox cheeks

8 ounces vermicelli rice noodles

1½ tablespoons butter

2 teaspoons ground cumin, plus extra for serving

2 teaspoons paprika , plus extra for serving

A small handful of finely chopped flat-leaf parsley leaves

Sea salt

One night in Fez, I was buying ingredients in the souk, which, as always, was buzzing with life—children running around, bicycles weaving through the crowds, busy shoppers elbowing past—all aglow in the light of a thousand yellow bulbs. The stalls lining the street were overflowing with fresh produce and sizzling food. I couldn't resist ducking into one little stall for a bite to eat. Two huge pots were steaming away, one containing several whole cows' heads. The stallholder pulled off some meat and served it to me with steamed noodles. Cumin and paprika were on the table for extra seasoning. It was super simple, but tasted incredible. I will admit that finding a whole cow's head and a steamer large enough to fit it is probably out of most people's culinary range, so here I have just used ox cheeks for a more accessible, home kitchen-friendly version. For me, it still conjures up some of the magic and bustle of Fez by night.

1. Place a steamer over medium-high heat, with enough water to last for about 4 hours. (You can always top up with more from the kettle if you need it.) Put the ox cheeks into the steamer. Cover and seal with aluminum foil and plastic wrap. Bring to a boil, then reduce the heat to low and steam for 3½ to 4 hours, or until you can pull the meat apart with a fork. Set aside to rest on a warm dish, covered.

2. Put the noodles into the water and cook for 8 to 10 minutes or until soft. Drain and transfer to a mixing bowl. Add the butter, season, and toss together.

3. To serve, put the noodles in a serving dish. Discard any fat from the ox cheeks and fork apart the meat. Season with salt, cumin, and paprika. Add to the dish with the noodles. Sprinkle over a little more cumin and paprika, and add the parsley. Serve immediately.

Harissa Beef Msemen

Makes 6 to 8 *msemen*

FOR THE DOUGH

2 cups all-purpose flour, plus extra for dusting

½ cup fine semolina flour

A pinch of salt

A pinch of sugar

¼ teaspoon active dried yeast

¾ cup plus 2 tablespoons warm water

5 tablespoons olive oil, 2 for greasing and the rest for frying

FOR THE FILLING

3 tablespoons olive oil

1 red onion, finely chopped

½ red pepper, deseeded and finely chopped

7 ounces ground beef

2 garlic cloves, thinly sliced

1 tomato, finely chopped

1 teaspoon ground cumin

½ teaspoon paprika

1 tablespoon harissa (page 183)

Juice of ¼ lemon

Sea salt

FOR THE HARISSA YOGURT

⅔ cup Greek yogurt

2 tablespoons harissa (page 183)

Pronounced *miss-i-men*, this flaky, buttery pancake can be found in different guises across North Africa and the Middle East. In Morocco, it is served with honey for breakfast, or found sizzling on hot plates in market stalls, stuffed with tomatoes or ground meat, like this version.

1. For the dough, use a fork to mix together the flour, semolina, salt, sugar, and yeast in a mixing bowl. Make a well in the center. Add about three-quarters of the water, and combine to form a dough, adding more water a tiny amount at a time, until you get a soft dough that's not too wet or sticky. Turn onto a floured surface and knead until smooth and shiny. Place in a lightly oiled bowl, cover, and leave for 20 minutes in a warm, dry place to rise.

2. Meanwhile, heat 3 tablespoons of oil in a large pan over high heat. Add the onion and pepper and stir-fry for 2 to 3 minutes, then add the beef and stir-fry for another 2 to 3 minutes. Add the garlic and stir-fry for 1 to 2 minutes more. Now add the tomato, cumin, paprika, a good pinch of salt, and a splash of water. Cook for 7 to 8 minutes, or until the tomato has broken down. Stir in the harissa paste and lemon juice. Transfer to a bowl and leave to cool.

3. Divide the risen dough into 6 to 8 equal pieces. Roll into balls and place, spaced well apart, on a lightly oiled baking sheet. Cover and leave for 20 minutes.

4. Take one of the dough balls and place on another oiled baking sheet. Turning the dough as you go, use your hands to spread it out into a circle. Flip it over so both sides are well oiled and continue to push out until it forms a thin disk, about 6 inches in diameter. Spread a few tablespoons of the beef mixture down the center, leaving space at the top and bottom. Fold in the sides and gently push down to seal. Now fold in the bottom and top edges, so that you have a square shape. Gently press down with your hands, turning as you go, until the square doubles in size. Repeat with the rest of the dough and filling.

5. Mix together the ingredients for the harissa yogurt and add some salt, then heat a tablespoon of the oil in a non-stick frying pan over high heat and cook the *msemen*, two at a time, for about a minute each side, or until golden and crispy. Place on paper towels to absorb any excess oil. Slice in half and serve immediately with the yogurt.

Fez Kefta Sandwich

Serves 2

2 tablespoons olive oil

½ red onion, finely chopped

½ pound ground beef

1 clove garlic

1 tomato, finely chopped

2 tablespoons tomato purée

2 tablespoons chile sauce, plus extra to serve

1 teaspoon *baharat* spice mix

½ cup pitted black olives, roughly chopped

A small handful of finely chopped flat-leaf parsley leaves

1 round Moroccan bread, cut into half moons, warmed, or crusty rolls of your choice

Lettuce, to serve

Sea salt

Fez has some of the best street food in Morocco, and as you weave your way through the narrow roads and winding alleyways, you discover more and more delicious snacks. This sandwich is a classic—ground meat cooked on a hot plate with onions, herbs, and spices, and served with masses of chile sauce in a soft, white roll. You can choose from lamb, beef, or merguez sausage, or even have a meat feast and mix all three. It's the ultimate speedy snack.

1. Heat the oil in a large frying pan over high heat. Add the onion and stir-fry for 2 to 3 minutes to soften, and then add the beef. Mix well and continue to stir-fry for 2 to 3 minutes until the meat is broken up and cooked.

2. Add the garlic and stir-fry for 10 seconds, until fragrant, then add the tomato and stir-fry for a minute to break it down.

3. Spoon in the tomato purée and add the chile sauce, *baharat*, and a good pinch of salt. Pour in 3 to 4 tablespoons of water to help mix everything together properly, and stir-fry for another 2 to 3 minutes to thicken. Add the olives and parsley and toss together into the beef.

4. Stuff the bread halves with lettuce and a generous helping of the beef. Top with more chile sauce if you're an addict like me, and serve immediately.

Sizzling Souk Kebabs

Serves 4
4 long skewers, soaked
in cold water if wooden

1¼ pounds lamb leg, cut into
1-inch cubes

2 to 3 ounces lamb fat, cut into
small pieces

½ red onion, grated

A small handful of finely
chopped flat-leaf parsley leaves

4 tablespoons olive oil

1 tablespoon cumin, plus extra
to serve

2 red onions, finely sliced

Juice of 1 lemon

Sea salt and freshly ground
black pepper

TO SERVE
2 tomatoes, sliced

Moroccan breads, or crusty
rolls of your choice

Harissa (page 183)

Brochettes, as these are known in Morocco, are
extremely popular. They can be found all year round in
the souks, but they are especially common during the
festival of Eid Al Adha, when the best cut of the lamb
is saved to make these succulent skewers. Ideally you
want to buy lean and tender meat from a young lamb,
around one to one and a half years old. To keep it juicy
with an incredibly intense flavor, little pieces of lamb fat
are threaded in between the meat, to melt over it during
cooking. You need to start preparing the lamb the day
before, so plan ahead.

1. Put the lamb and lamb fat into a mixing bowl and add the
grated onion. Its pulpy consistency helps to flavor and tenderize
the meat, and it will caramelize later on the barbecue. Add the
parsley and a good pinch of salt and pepper. Mix well. Cover and
refrigerate overnight.

2. Heat the barbecue. Pour the olive oil over the meat and mix
well. Thread onto skewers, alternating meat with a little fat. Once
at room temperature, barbecue for 1 to 2 minutes each side,
turning four times, seasoning each time with a pinch of cumin
and a tiny pinch of salt, until beautifully golden and still a little
pink in the middle. Transfer to a warm serving dish, cover with
foil, and rest for 5 minutes.

3. Meanwhile, put the sliced onions into a mixing bowl. Pour over
the lemon juice and season with salt. Mix well and set aside to
soften for 5 to 10 minutes.

4. Serve the kebabs with the onions and tomatoes in bowls, as
well as bread, harissa, and more cumin, black pepper, and salt
for seasoning.

Marrakesh Lamb Tangia

Serves 2

2 teaspoons cumin seeds

4 preserved lemons, whole (page 184)

6 garlic cloves, peeled

A handful of cilantro leaves and stems

A handful of flat-leaf parsley leaves and stems

A small pinch of saffron

1 teaspoon ras el hanout (see note on page 180)

2 tablespoons butter

3 tablespoons olive oil

2 lamb shanks (about 14 ounces each)

Sea salt and freshly ground black pepper

TO SERVE

Green olives tossed in harissa

Moroccan bread, or crusty rolls of your choice

Cumin salt (page 180)

Mint tea (page 179)

Tangia is a classic Marrakesh dish of slow-cooked lamb with fermented butter known as *smen*, spices, and preserved lemons. It is made in a pear-shaped earthenware pot called a *tangia*. These deep, narrow pots are used to braise meat slowly in the embers of a fire. The soft, unctuous meat is served with bread, harissa-flavored olives, and mint tea. This type of meal is one of life's great pleasures and its perfumed perfection is easy to re-create at home: put everything into a well-sealed saucepan, slow cook for hours, and let the alchemy happen. Here I have used ordinary butter rather than *smen*, to make the ingredients easy to source.

1. Preheat the oven to 500°F. Toast the cumin seeds in a dry pan over low heat until fragrant. Cool and grind into a powder.

2. Select an ovenproof pot or saucepan that will fit the lamb shanks snugly. Put the lemons, garlic, cilantro, parsley, saffron, ras el hanout, butter, oil, and 1½ cups water into the pot, then add the ground cumin seeds and season well. Mix together. Add the lamb shanks to the pot and push into the liquid.

3. Cut a round of parchment paper to fit the inside of the pot. Scrunch it up under the cold tap, smooth out, and lay snugly over the meat. Cover with a large sheet of foil and top with the pot lid. Scrunch the sides of the foil together to seal the rim of the pot and the lid. This will help keep as much moisture in the pot as possible, ensuring the meat is meltingly tender.

4. Transfer the pot to the oven and immediately reduce the temperature to 325°F. Cook for 5 hours, or until the meat pulls apart easily at the touch of a fork.

5. Take off the lid and heat on the stovetop over medium heat for 3 to 4 minutes so that the sauce thickens a little. Remove from the heat, cover with the lid, and set aside to rest for 10 minutes. Pour off the excess fat and turn everything into a warm serving dish. Discard the herbs and serve immediately with the harissa olives, bread, cumin salt, and mint tea.

Harira Soup

Serves 4 to 6

2 teaspoons cumin seeds

8 tablespoons olive oil

2 onions, finely chopped

3 celery sticks, finely chopped

2 carrots, finely chopped

6 garlic cloves, finely chopped

2 teaspoons ground ginger

1 teaspoon ground cinnamon

½ teaspoon ground black pepper

½ teaspoon ground turmeric

14-ounce can chopped tomatoes

4 tablespoons tomato purée

15-ounce can chickpeas, drained and rinsed

¼ cup Basmati rice

1 cup green lentils

A handful of flat-leaf parsley leaves

A handful of cilantro leaves

1 quart vegetable stock

Zest and juice of 1 lemon

⅓ cup walnuts

Sea salt

Traditionally cooked to break the fast during Ramadan, these days this thick soup is cooked all the time all over the country, and eaten as a light lunch or quick snack before dinner. The particular flavors and ingredients vary regionally, but generally it is made with chickpeas and a carbohydrate such as potatoes. The soup probably has its origins in a semolina-based dish eaten by the Berbers in the High Atlas. The tomatoes would have been added with the advent of New World foods. My version is vegetarian, using chickpeas, rice, and lentils. For a pop of freshness, I add a walnut gremolata at the end.

1. Begin by toasting the cumin seeds to bring out the flavor. Place a frying pan over medium heat. Add the cumin seeds and reduce the heat to low. Toast the seeds, shaking the pan occasionally, for 3 to 3½ minutes. Cool, then grind into a fine powder.

2. Heat 4 tablespoons of oil in a large casserole over medium heat. Add the onions, celery, and carrots, and cook, stirring occasionally, for 10 to 12 minutes or until soft and sticky. Add the garlic, mix well, and cook for 10 seconds until fragrant. Add the toasted cumin, along with the ginger, cinnamon, black pepper, and turmeric, and a big pinch of salt. Mix well and cook for a few seconds until the aroma of the spices fills your kitchen.

3. Pour the tomatoes and tomato purée into the pan. Add the chickpeas, rice, lentils, and half the herbs and pour over the stock. Mix well. Bring to a boil, cover, reduce the heat to low and simmer for 20 minutes, or until the lentils are soft and the rice cooked. Check the seasoning and add half the lemon juice. Mix together.

4. Meanwhile, heat a small frying pan over medium heat and toast the walnuts for 5 to 6 minutes, shaking the pan occasionally, to intensify their flavors. Remove from the heat and leave to cool. Place in a food processor and add the remaining flat-leaf parsley and cilantro. Blend until fine. Transfer to a mixing bowl. Pour in the remaining oil and add the lemon zest and the remaining juice. Season with a good pinch of salt and mix well.

5. Serve the soup in bowls with some of the walnut gremolata spooned on top.

Bissara Soup

Serves 4 to 6

1 pound dried split fava beans, soaked overnight

8 garlic cloves, crushed

1 tablespoon ground cumin, plus extra to serve

1 tablespoon paprika, plus extra to serve

2 tablespoons olive oil, plus extra for drizzling

Sea salt

This protein-packed, energy-boosting soup is a staple Moroccan breakfast dish. Traditionally, it is eaten during the cold winter months, but so loved is the creamy consistency that it can be found all over the country, all the time. The dried beans are cooked in garlic and spices until thick and rich, and then served with a slick of peppery olive oil and a few warming spices. It's incredibly comforting, deeply nourishing, and deceptively filling. (Picture on page 27.)

1. Wash the soaked beans in cold water several times to make sure they are clean. Drain well. Place in a pan and pour in enough cold water to cover the beans by about ½ inch. Bring to a boil over high heat, and remove any scum with a slotted spoon.

2. Put the garlic, cumin, paprika, and oil in the pan and mix well. Bring to a boil, then reduce the heat to low. Cover and cook for 1 hour to 1 hour 20 minutes, or until the beans are falling apart. You will need to top up the water levels occasionally so that the beans are just covered, never fully exposed. Stir every now and again.

3. Season with a really good pinch of salt and blend until smooth using a hand-held stick blender. To serve, divide the soup into bowls, drizzle with olive oil, and add a good pinch of cumin, salt, and paprika.

Steamed Chickpea Baguettes

Serves 4

8 ounces dried chickpeas
4 small white rolls/baguettes
7 oz cream cheese
4 teaspoons ground cumin
2 teaspoons chile powder
Sea salt

Weaving through the busy streets of Fez is hungry work, and those in the know head to the winding alleyways of Nejjarine for their street food fix. Bustling stalls and little carts sell all manner of deliciousness, including these chickpea baguettes. The soaked chickpeas are steamed until soft, then seasoned to within an inch of their lives with salt, musty Moroccan cumin, and chile powder, and stuffed into a soft baguette that has been slathered with cream cheese. It's a heavenly combination of flavors and textures, and perfect fuel for the day.

1. Soak the chickpeas overnight in a large pan of cold water. Drain, rinse thoroughly, and drain again.

2. Place a tight-fitting colander or steamer over a large pan filled with water. Wrap foil over the joint between the pan and colander to help trap the steam. Heat the pan over high heat until boiling and steaming. Turn the chickpeas into the colander, cover, and reduce the heat to low. Steam for 2½ to 3 hours, mixing the chickpeas every hour until tender.

3. Meanwhile, preheat the oven to 350°F and warm the rolls or baguettes through. Cut open and spread a generous amount of cream cheese inside.

4. Toss the chickpeas in the cumin, chile powder, and salt and stuff into a warm baguette. Serve immediately.

Batbout Breakfast Bread with Butter & Honey

Makes 5
breads

1 (¼-ounce) packet active dry yeast

1 teaspoon sugar

1¾ cups warm water

1 cup plus 2 tablespoons fine semolina flour

2½ cups all-purpose flour, plus extra for dusting

4 tablespoons olive oil, plus extra for oiling the sheet

Sea salt

TO SERVE

Good-quality extra virgin olive oil or butter

Honey

This simple recipe reminds me of sitting at a faded blue table in a tiny alleyway in Essaouira on Morocco's Atlantic coast. The chef cooked *batbout*, a pillowy soft round bread, on a piping hot griddle right in front of me, expertly flipping each one several times as they puffed up and rose, so they took on a little color without burning. Olive oil and honey were poured generously over the bread as it was served. This comforting combo is the on-the-go breakfast of Morocco, available in various guises across the country; in the south they mix olive oil and honey, and in the north it's butter. Either way, I love the simplicity of it.

1. Put the yeast into a large measuring cup. Add the sugar and pour in the water. Whisk together and leave for 8 to 10 minutes to froth.

2. Put the semolina into a large mixing bowl. Add a good pinch of salt and sift over the flour. Pour the olive oil into the bowl and slowly add the yeast liquid, a little at a time, combining as you go to form a dough. You may not need all the liquid.

3. Once the dough forms, and starts coming together, turn it out onto a floured surface and knead for about 10 minutes, or until really shiny and soft. Divide into 5 pieces, shape into small balls, and place, spaced well apart, on an oiled baking sheet. Cover and leave to rise for about 30 minutes. On a floured work surface, roll out each ball into a round pizza shape about $^1/_{10}$-inch thick and then leave, covered with a clean cloth, for an hour to rise.

4. Heat a non-stick frying pan over medium-high heat and cook the *batbout* one at a time for about 2 minutes each side, then cook for a further 1 minute each side to allow the center to cook properly. Reduce the heat if necessary. The bread will puff up and turn golden. If it needs more time for the dough to cook, allow a further 30 seconds to 1 minute a side until done. Keep warm while you cook the rest of the breads.

5. Serve with a choice of olive oil or butter and honey.

Beghrir Pancakes

Makes 10 to 12
little pancakes

1 cup warm water
½ packet (about 1 teaspoon)
active dry yeast
½ teaspoon sugar
1 cup full-fat milk
2 free-range eggs
¾ cup fine semolina flour
1¼ cups all-purpose flour
2 teaspoons baking powder
A pinch of salt
3 tablespoons butter, for frying

TO SERVE
Honey
Jam
Nut butter

Known as "pancakes with a million holes," these muffin-like crêpes are soft, spongy, and delicious. Made with yeast, they are also fluffy and light. *Beghrir* are cooked in homes across the country for a pre-dawn breakfast during Ramadan, and often served with butter and honey, which they joyously soak up. You also find them piled high in souks and markets, perfect for a snack during a busy shopping spree. I love mine piping hot, with Moroccan nut butter *(amlou)*.

1. Pour the warm water into a large measuring cup and add the yeast and sugar. Whisk together and leave for a few minutes until foaming. Add the milk and whisk in the eggs.

2. Put the semolina, flour, baking powder, and salt into a bowl. Mix well and slowly pour in the liquid mixture, whisking as you go, until it's all combined into a smooth batter. Cover and set aside for 30 minutes so that the yeast aerates the mixture.

3. Heat some of the butter in a small non-stick frying pan over medium heat. Pour in 4 to 5 tablespoons of the batter and cook for about 3½ to 4 minutes, or until the surface is pitted with holes like honeycomb, and the surface looks set and matte colored rather than shiny. *Beghrir* are only cooked on one side so you need to adjust the heat to ensure the bottom does not burn before the top is cooked. Put the cooked pancake onto a warm serving dish and cover. Repeat with the remaining batter.

4. Serve the pancakes with honey, jam, and nut butter so that everyone can pick their favorite topping.

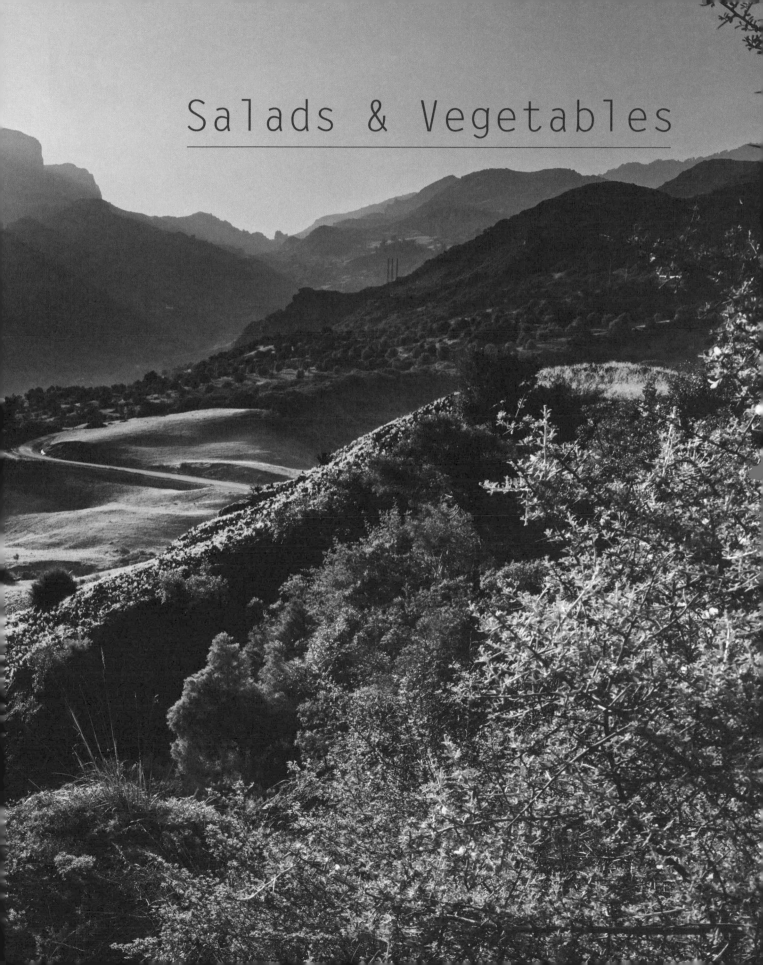

Salads & Vegetables

Chicken, Preserved Lemon, & Olive Salad

Serves 4

2 garlic cloves

½ teaspoon ground cumin

½ teaspoon ground coriander

¼ teaspoon ground ginger

¼ teaspoon ground turmeric

4½ tablespoons olive oil

Juice of 2½ lemons

1¼ pounds boneless skinless chicken thighs

1 cup couscous

½ red onion, finely chopped

1 fennel bulb, finely sliced

14-ounce can chickpeas, drained and rinsed

1 preserved lemon (see page 184), pith discarded and zest finely chopped

¾ cup pitted green olives, roughly chopped

A handful of finely chopped cilantro leaves, plus a small handful of leaves to garnish

A handful of finely chopped mint leaves

Sea salt

Chicken tagine with preserved lemons and olives is one of the most well-known dishes from Morocco. With the recipe so readily available, I felt it didn't warrant another—but the flavors are an essential part of Moroccan cuisine. So I started to experiment with it, and this is my interpretation: a modern, zingy salad inspired by the traditional version. The signature flavors of tagine became a marinade for the meat, and the other ingredients— olives, preserved lemons, couscous, herbs—form the salad. This is perfect for a summer supper with a cold glass of vino and if the weather's lousy, it will bring a little of that hazy heat from the dusty hills of Morocco to brighten up your home.

1. Using a mortar and pestle, mash the garlic into a paste with a little salt. Add the cumin, ground coriander, ginger, turmeric, two tablespoons of the olive oil, and the juice of ½ lemon and mix well. Put the chicken in a mixing bowl and add the spice paste. Mix everything together really well so that the chicken thighs are completely coated. Cover and refrigerate for 1 hour or overnight.

2. Put the couscous into a small bowl and pour over enough warm water to cover by about ¼ inch. Cover the bowl with plastic wrap.

3. Put the red onion in a small mixing bowl, then add the juice of ½ lemon and a small pinch of salt. Toss together and leave for a few minutes to mellow the rawness of the onion. Add the fennel and ½ tablespoon of olive oil and toss together.

4. Put the couscous in a large mixing bowl. Add the chickpeas, fennel and onion, preserved lemon, olives, herbs, juice of 1 lemon, and 2 tablespoons of olive oil. Mix everything together really well.

5. Meanwhile preheat the broiler to 500°F or its highest setting. Place the chicken on a foil-covered broiler pan and broil for 7 to 8 minutes each side or until cooked through and a little golden. Once cooked, slice into thin strips, season with a little salt, and squeeze over the juice of ½ lemon.

6. To serve, turn the salad out onto a large platter. Arrange the chicken over the top and spoon over any juices left in the pan. Garnish with cilantro leaves and serve immediately.

Goat Cheese & Grapefruit Salad

Serves 2
as a light lunch

3½ ounces ciabatta or sourdough bread (slightly stale is best)

2 tablespoons olive oil

2 oranges

2 pink grapefruits

Juice of ½ lemon

3½ ounces arugula leaves

2 ounces mâche

¼ cup walnuts, smashed

4 ounces soft goat cheese

1 tablespoon argan oil

Sea salt and freshly ground black pepper

Morocco is not well known for its cheese, but on the edge of the Bouhachem Forest in the north, the goat farmers take their milk to local cooperatives who produce fantastic varieties of cheese. They make a soft, round cheese called *chaouen* (Berber for goat's horn) and a light, spreadable cheese called *jben*, which is used on everything from pancakes to salads. This simple salad would be a great way to enjoy *jben*, dotted onto a variety of citrus fruits and arugula leaves. You can use any soft goat cheese you like. And if you can't find argan oil, try using hazelnut or peanut oil instead.

1. Preheat the oven to 350°F. Rip the bread into bite-sized pieces and put into a roasting pan. Drizzle with the olive oil and bake for 5 to 6 minutes until golden brown. Set aside to cool.

2. Segment the oranges and grapefruits over a mixing bowl to catch the juices as you go. Add the lemon juice and a pinch of salt. Put the salad leaves into the bowl and toss together. Arrange on a serving plate and spoon over the juices.

3. Scatter the bread and walnuts over the top, and dollop over the soft cheese. Drizzle over the argan oil and add a pinch of pepper to the goat cheese. Serve immediately.

Cauliflower, Fennel, Orange, & Saffron Salad

Serves 2
as a light lunch
or starter

FOR THE RAISIN
DRESSING
4 tablespoons cider vinegar
4 teaspoons sugar
½ cup golden raisins
A small pinch of saffron threads
½ teaspoon orange blossom
water
Sea salt

FOR THE SALAD
1 pound cauliflower florets
1 fennel bulb
2 oranges
A handful of roughly
chopped mint leaves
A handful of finely chopped
flat-leaf parsley leaves
Juice of 1 lemon
2 tablespoons olive oil
2 tablespoons roasted blanched
almonds, lightly crushed into
pieces

Modern Moroccan food is so exciting. Creative chefs are reinterpreting traditional dishes and giving authentic flavors a different spin. I took inspiration from them to develop this salad. The cauliflower is lightly blanched to make it more palatable, and served with freshly shaved fennel and herbs. But it's the dressing that's really special—a simple vinaigrette base, infused with saffron and orange blossom. Golden raisins are added, which wake up and swell in these floral flavors, adding sweetness. The golden yellow of the saffron bleeds into the dressing and coats everything with its riotous color.

1. Begin by making the dressing. Pour the vinegar and sugar into a small saucepan and add the raisins. Bring to a boil over medium heat and dissolve the sugar, shaking the pan occasionally. Reduce the heat to low and add the saffron, orange blossom water, and a pinch of salt. Mix together and cook for 6 to 8 minutes, stirring occasionally, or until the raisins are really swollen and the sauce is sticky. Remove from the heat and set aside to let the beautiful flavors infuse even more.

2. Blanch the cauliflower in boiling water for about 4 to 5 minutes, drain and refresh in cold water, then drain again.

3. Finely slice the cauliflower and shave the fennel super-fine (a mandolin is useful here). Segment the oranges over a bowl to catch the juices. Put all three ingredients in a serving dish with the juices, mint, and parsley. Add the raisins and all the fragrant, sticky syrup from the pan. Pour in the lemon juice and olive oil, and season well with salt. Toss the salad together so everything gets coated in the syrup and light dressing. Finally scatter the almonds over the top and serve immediately.

Naima's Grilled Vegetables

Serves 4

8 tablespoons olive oil, plus
2 teaspoons for the peppers

3 eggplants, sliced
lengthwise into thin strips

2 red peppers

Juice of ½ lemon

2 garlic cloves, thinly sliced

4 tomatoes, peeled, seeds
squeezed out, and flesh
roughly chopped

1 tablespoon tomato purée

1 teaspoon ground cumin

½ teaspoon paprika

A pinch of sugar

A small handful of roughly
chopped mint leaves

Extra virgin olive oil, for
drizzling

Sea salt and freshly ground
black pepper

My friend, photographer Alan Keohane, has lived in Morocco for many years, taking fabulous pictures of the Berber tribes. He accompanied me on one of my recent trips to the country, and took the location photographs for this book. Alan introduced me to his assistant, Naima, and her sister, Kabira, who were both fantastic cooks. They made this for me when I stayed in their village, Toughana, south of Marrakesh. It was delicious—real home cooking at its best.

1. Heat a grill pan or cast-iron skillet over high heat until smoking. Brush around 6 tablespoons of the oil over the eggplant slices. Season with salt and grill in batches, for 2 to 3 minutes each side, until charred and tender.

2. Meanwhile carefully cook the peppers over a medium-high gas flame on the stovetop, using tongs to turn them as you go, for about 10 to 12 minutes, until completely charred and tender. (Alternatively, run the peppers under a broiler, turning, until completely charred.) You should be able to poke a skewer into the charred skin and straight through the flesh. Place in a bowl and cover with plastic wrap. Leave to cool. Once cool, discard the burned skin, chop off the tops, and scoop out the seeds. Finely chop the flesh and transfer to a mixing bowl. Add 2 teaspoons of olive oil, a pinch of salt, and the lemon juice. Mix well and set aside.

3. Heat the remaining oil in a pan over medium heat. Add the garlic and cook for 30 seconds until fragrant. Add the chopped tomatoes, tomato purée, cumin, paprika, sugar, and a good pinch of salt and pepper. Mix together, and cook for 8 to 10 minutes, stirring occasionally, until thick. Leave to cool.

4. To serve, arrange the cooked eggplants on a serving plate, spoon over the tomato sauce, and top with the peppers. Scatter with the mint and drizzle with a little extra virgin olive oil. Serve immediately.

Mixed Vegetable Salad

Serves 4
as a side dish

4 beets, washed, peeled
and cut into little wedges

2 zucchini, trimmed and cut into
¾-inch pieces

3 garlic cloves

4 tablespoons olive oil

Juice of ½ lemon

½ teaspoon ground cumin

A handful of finely chopped
flat-leaf parsley leaves

Sea salt and freshly ground
black pepper

This simple dish is a variation on the classic Moroccan salads, where the individual veggies are boiled until tender and tossed in a dressing. They would be served as part of a meze starter, before a big meal, or served as a side dish to a simple tagine. Rather than boiling, I favor roasting the vegetables to intensify their flavors before dressing them in lemon juice and olive oil.

1. Preheat the oven to 425°F. Put the beets, zucchini, and garlic in a small roasting pan. Pour in half the olive oil and season with salt and pepper. Mix together and roast for 50 to 60 minutes until tender. Remove from the oven and leave to cool for a few minutes.

2. Remove the garlic cloves. Pop the cloves out of their skins and into a small mixing bowl. Add the lemon juice, remaining olive oil, cumin, and a good pinch of salt. Mash together with a fork to create a dressing. Pour the dressing over the cooked vegetables and gently toss together. Scatter with the parsley and serve warm.

Tomato & Red Onion Salad

Serves 4
as part of a meal

2 tomatoes, peeled, seeds
squeezed out, and flesh finely
chopped

1 red onion, finely chopped

1 garlic clove, mashed using a
mortar and pestle or the flat side
of a knife blade

A pinch of ground cumin

Juice of ½ lemon

2 to 3 tablespoons olive oil

Sea salt

This is the basic side salad of Morocco, served in restaurants, cafes, and homes all over the country to accompany a main meal. The main ingredients, plump tomatoes and sweet red onions, are found growing in abundance all over the country, so it's a natural for a quick salad. The juices are perfect for cutting through rich tagines and grilled meat, and are delicious mopped up with fresh bread.

Put everything into a serving dish. Toss together and serve immediately.

Atlas Mountain Salad

Serves 4
as a part of a meal

1 red onion, finely chopped

Juice of 1 lemon

2 tomatoes, peeled, seeds squeezed out, and flesh finely chopped

1 cucumber, peeled, seeded, and finely chopped

1 red pepper, seeded, and finely chopped

¾ cup pomegranate seeds

3 tablespoons olive oil

A small handful of mint leaves

Sea salt

While passing through the Atlas Mountains to get to the desert, I stopped off for lunch in a small café in the rather unusually named Taddart 2, a tiny dot of a village on the mountain pass. I ordered lamb cutlets and tea. The food arrived with this vibrant salad; a crunchy mix of onion, cucumber, pepper, and pomegranate seeds, doused in a zesty dressing. It was divine and cut through the richness of the lamb perfectly. It's easy to make and looks so vibrant. I love to serve this with grilled fish, lamb, or a rich tagine, and loads of bread to mop up the juices.

1. Put the onion into a small mixing bowl. Squeeze over the lemon juice and add a pinch of salt—this will take some of the bite out of the onions. Mix well and leave for 5 to 10 minutes while you prepare all the other ingredients.

2. Put the tomatoes, cucumber, pepper, and pomegranate seeds in a serving dish. Add the onions and the juice, olive oil, and a small pinch of salt. Mix well. Garnish with the mint leaves and serve immediately.

Zaalouk with Crispy Halloumi

Serves 4

3 large eggplants

5 tablespoons olive oil, plus extra for drizzling

4 garlic cloves, finely chopped

4 tomatoes, finely chopped

2 tablespoons tomato purée

2 teaspoons ground cumin

2 teaspoons paprika

½ teaspoon dried chile flakes

1 bay leaf

A pinch of sugar

Juice of ¼ lemon

A handful of finely chopped cilantro leaves

10 ounces halloumi, cut into thin slices

Warm pita, to serve (or try it with *batbout*, page 30)

Sea salt

Zaalouk is served at room temperature as a side dish. The eggplant is first cooked over a flame until charred and tender and then added to a thick tomato sauce and finished off with olive oil, lemon juice, and chopped flat-leaf parsley. It's perfect for dunking, so get plenty of soft warm pita lined up. To make this into more of a meal, I like to serve my *zaalouk* with pieces of crispy, pan-fried halloumi. Although it's not really Moroccan, the salty cheese works so well with the richness of the eggplants that it's a perfect pairing.

1. Prick the eggplants all over with a skewer. Carefully place each one over a medium gas flame and cook for 3 to 4 minutes each side, turning four times, or until tender. (Alternatively, you can roast the eggplants in a 500°F oven, turning occasionally, until charred and collapsed.) You should be able to poke a skewer into the charred skin and straight through the flesh when they are cooked. Remove from the heat and leave to cool. Once cool to the touch, remove and discard the burned skin. Cut off the top and finely chop the flesh. Set aside.

2. Meanwhile, heat 3 tablespoons of the oil in a pan over medium heat. Add the garlic and cook for 30 seconds until fragrant. Stir in the tomatoes, tomato purée, cumin, paprika, chile flakes, bay leaf, and sugar. Season with a good pinch of salt. Add ½ cup of water, mix well, and bring to a boil. Cover, reduce the heat to low, and cook for 10 to 12 minutes, stirring occasionally, or until the tomatoes have broken down.

3. Transfer the eggplant to the tomato sauce. Mix well and check the seasoning. Cover and cook for a further 10 to 12 minutes, stirring occasionally, or until the sauce is lovely and thick. Add the lemon juice and cilantro and mix together.

4. While the eggplant cook in the sauce, heat the remaining oil in a large frying pan over medium heat. Carefully place the halloumi slices in the pan and cook for 1 to 2 minutes each side until golden and crispy.

5. To serve, spread the *zaalouk* in a serving dish and top with halloumi. Drizzle with olive oil and serve immediately with pita.

Seven-Vegetable Couscous

Serves 4 to 6

2 tablespoons olive oil

2 red onions, finely chopped

3 garlic cloves, finely chopped

4 tomatoes, finely chopped

3 tablespoons tomato purée

2 teaspoons ground cumin

2 teaspoons ground ginger

1½ teaspoons paprika

A small pinch of saffron threads

2 carrots, halved lengthwise and cut into 2-inch strips

8 ounces new potatoes, halved

6 ounces baby zucchini, some halved lengthwise

8 ounces baby turnips, washed, peeled and halved

1 bulb fennel, cut into 8 wedges

1½ cups vegetable stock

½ small cabbage (8 ounces), cored and cut into wedges

1 red pepper, seeded and cut into 6 pieces

A small handful of finely chopped cilantro leaves

10 ounces couscous

I first tasted this celebratory dish in a stunning *riad* in Fez. My hostess Souad had invited me to join her family for their traditional Friday meal. Souad had prepared a mountain of couscous, piled high with spicy stewed vegetables. Some families cook the vegetables with lamb, and others without, and sometimes a *tfaya*—cinnamon-spiced raisins and onions (page 73)—tops the dish. Food and family are what make life worth living, and it was so special to be scooped up by my wonderful hostess to join her family while I was away from mine.

1. Heat the olive oil in a large, shallow pan over medium heat. Add the onions and cook, stirring occasionally, for 4 to 5 minutes until a little golden. Add the garlic and cook for 10 seconds until fragrant. Add the chopped tomatoes, tomato purée, cumin, ginger, paprika, saffron, and a good pinch of salt and pepper. Mix well.

2. Put the carrots, potatoes, zucchini, turnips, and fennel in the pan. Pour over the stock, mix together, and bring to a boil. Cover, reduce the heat to low, and cook for 30 minutes to soften. Push the cabbage and pepper into the sauce. Cover and cook for a further 20 to 25 minutes until everything is tender. Check the seasoning, stir in the cilantro and mix well.

3. Meanwhile, put the couscous in a bowl. Season with salt and pepper, and pour over enough just-boiled water to cover by about ¼ inch. Cover with plastic wrap and set aside until the water has been absorbed.

4. Fluff the couscous with a fork and turn out into a huge serving dish. Make a well in the center and fill it with the vegetables. Spoon over some of sauce, and pour the rest into a little serving dish. Serve the couscous immediately with the extra sauce on the table.

Herby Couscous Salad

Serves 4

1⅓ cups couscous

6 tablespoons olive oil

1 red onion, finely chopped

1 red pepper, finely chopped

2½ teaspoons paprika

2 teaspoons ground cumin

A large bunch of finely chopped flat-leaf parsley leaves

3 handfuls of finely chopped chives

Juice of 1½ lemons

1 preserved lemon (page 184), seeded and finely chopped

Sea salt and freshly ground black pepper

Deep in the desert, in a small village called Tagenza, my friend Aicha, a wonderful Berber woman, cooked me a feast that included this special couscous dish. She prepared the couscous traditionally, washing and steaming it three times. However, on the last round, she added a mix of herbs, onions, and spices that had been pan-fried in oil. This was mixed into the couscous as she massaged the grains using her fingers before the final steaming. The flavors permeated the green-flecked semolina. The biggest surprise was the chives; most un-Moroccan, I thought. But no, they grew all over the garden, and the delicate allium tang perfumed the salad in just the right way.

1. Put the couscous in a large bowl and pour over just enough boiled water to cover by about ¼ inch. Cover with plastic wrap and set aside. Or, if you want to do this the traditional way and steam the couscous, see page 186.

2. Meanwhile, heat 4 tablespoons of the olive oil in a frying pan over medium heat. Add the onion and pepper and cook, stirring occasionally, for 6 to 8 minutes until soft. Add the paprika, cumin, parsley, chives, and a good pinch of salt. Mix well and cook for 30 seconds so that the herbs soften. Add the lemon juice and mix well. Remove from the heat.

3. Fluff the couscous with a fork and add the vegetables. Add the preserved lemon and the remaining oil. Toss together. Cover and leave to cool for 5 to 10 minutes—this helps the flavors develop. Check the seasoning and transfer to a serving dish. Serve immediately.

Berber Frittata

Serves 4

2 tablespoons butter

1 tablespoon olive oil

1 onion, finely sliced

2 red peppers, seeded and finely sliced

4 garlic cloves, finely sliced

2 tomatoes, finely chopped

2 tablespoons tomato purée

¾ cup pitted black olives, roughly chopped

1 teaspoon paprika

¼ teaspoon ground cinnamon

2 teaspoons ground cumin, plus a pinch for the eggs

1 teaspoon ground black pepper

1 teaspoon ground ginger

A large handful of finely chopped cilantro leaves

6 free-range eggs

6 tablespoons grated Cheddar cheese

Sea salt

The Atlas Mountains are a huge draw for avid trekkers looking for challenging peaks and spectacular scenery— as well as for wandering chefs in search of authentic Berber cuisine. I was staying in a tiny village called Tacheddirt to learn about traditional barbecue, and on my last night there, a trekking guide named Abdul arrived at my friend's house, starving hungry. He knocked up a frittata made with spiced vegetables, herbs, olives, and eggs. Served with masses of soft bread, it was perfect for anyone who had had a long day on the mountain. And if you're not on the mountains, it's superb served with a fresh salad as a light lunch.

1. Preheat the oven to 425°F. Melt the butter and oil in a large, ovenproof non-stick frying pan over medium heat. Add the onion and peppers and cook, stirring occasionally, for 8 to 10 minutes until soft and a little golden, adding the garlic half way.

2. Put the tomatoes, tomato purée, olives, and all the spices into the pan. Season with a good pinch of salt and add ½ cup of water. Mix everything together and cook, stirring occasionally, for 5 to 6 minutes until nice and thick, adding more water if the pan gets too dry. Stir in the cilantro and mix well.

3. Meanwhile, crack the eggs into a mixing bowl and season with salt and a pinch of cumin. Pour over the peppers and half mix, half shake the pan so that the eggs settle into the vegetables. Cook for 3 to 4 minutes, until the eggs start to set around the sides and little bubbles begin to appear on the surface. Scatter over the cheese and pop into the oven for 5 to 6 minutes, or until the eggs have just set and the molten cheese is a little golden. Leave to cool for a few minutes in the pan, then run a spatula around the sides and slide onto a board to serve.

Rabartahro Soup

Serves 4

1 winter squash (about 2 pounds), peeled, seeded and cut into 1-inch cubes

6 tablespoons olive oil

2 red onions, finely chopped

3 garlic cloves, roughly chopped

2 tomatoes, roughly chopped

1½ teaspoons ground cumin

1½ teaspoons ground ginger

3⅓ cups vegetable stock

¼ cup bulgur wheat

Juice of ½ lemon

A handful of roughly chopped cilantro leaves

A handful of roughly chopped flat-leaf parsley leaves

Sea salt and freshly ground black pepper

Rabartahro is a traditional soup made in autumn when pumpkin and squash are in season. The vegetables are cooked slowly with bulgur wheat. It is a little sweet and gently spiced, a perfect, hearty, warming dish to fight off the cold night air. For my version, I've added a fragrant herb oil at the end for a pop of freshness and color. This is Moroccan mountain food at its best.

1. Preheat the oven to 425°F. Spread the squash out on a roasting pan. Drizzle with 2 tablespoons of olive oil and season well with salt and pepper. Mix together and roast for 40 to 45 minutes until golden and tender.

2. Meanwhile, heat 2 tablespoons of the olive oil in a large pan over medium heat. Add the onion and cook, stirring occasionally, for 4 to 5 minutes until a little golden. Add two-thirds of the chopped garlic and cook for 10 seconds until fragrant.

3. Put the tomatoes in the pan. Mix well, and cook, stirring occasionally, for 2 to 3 minutes so they start to break down. Add the cumin, ginger, and a good pinch of salt and pepper. Mix well. Pour in the stock and bring to a boil.

4. Transfer the cooked squash to the pan, and blend until smooth using a hand-held stick blender.

5. Add the bulgur wheat to the pan and mix well. Bring to a boil, cover, reduce the heat to low, and cook for 15 to 20 minutes until the bulgur is tender. Check the seasoning and add the lemon juice. Mix well.

6. Meanwhile, put the remaining garlic into a mortar with a pinch of salt. Grind into a paste. Add the herbs and grind again to form a smooth paste. Add a pinch of pepper and the remaining olive oil. Mix well.

7. To serve, spoon the soup into bowls and add a dollop of the herb oil to each one.

La3dass

Serves 4
as a meze or side

3 tablespoons plus
1 teaspoon olive oil

2 red onions, finely sliced

2 garlic cloves, finely sliced

2 tomatoes, roughly chopped

2 tablespoons tomato purée

2 teaspoons paprika

1 teaspoon ground cumin

½ teaspoon ground black
pepper

A small bunch of finely
chopped flat-leaf parsley
leaves

1 cup dried green lentils

Sea salt

The Moroccan name for this dish looks unusual in Western lettering: *la3dass*. The "3" is used in place of an Arabic letter the Roman alphabet doesn't have. Pronounced *la-ha-diss*, meaning lentils, this simple braised dish is an everyday family meal that would be served with bread and perhaps some fried fish. It's hearty winter food made using dried pulses and spices—perfect for a cold night. I also had *la3dass* in Fez, braised with cured meat or *khlea*, which gave the dish an extra richness as the meat melted through the sauce.

1. Heat 3 tablespoons of oil in a pan over medium heat and add the onions. Cook for 10 to 12 minutes, stirring occasionally, until golden and caramelized. Add the garlic, mix well, and cook for 10 seconds until fragrant. Remove a quarter of the onion and garlic mix and reserve for a garnish.

2. Put the tomatoes, tomato purée, spices, and half the parsley into the pan, and mix well. Add the lentils and 3 cups of just-boiled water. Bring to a boil, cover, reduce the heat to low and cook for 1 hour, or until the lentils are tender. Remove the lid and turn the heat up to medium. Season well, and cook, stirring occasionally, for 10 to 15 minutes, or until the lentils have absorbed all the liquid.

3. Meanwhile heat the remaining oil in a small non-stick frying pan over high heat. Add the reserved onion and garlic mixture and season with a pinch of salt. Stir-fry for 2 to 3 minutes until crisp, then drain on paper towels.

4. To serve, turn the lentils out into a warm dish and scatter over the crispy onions and remaining parsley.

Harissa Carrots

Serves 4
as part of a meze

1 pound carrots, peeled and sliced into ½-inch pieces

1 garlic clove

¼ teaspoon ground cumin

½ teaspoon paprika

2 teaspoons harissa (page 183)

1 tablespoon red wine vinegar

2 tablespoons olive oil

A handful of finely chopped cilantro leaves

Sea salt and freshly ground black pepper

Originally from the kitchens of Fez, a traditional Moroccan carrot salad would have been served sweet, with plenty of cinnamon and sugar, for an opulent side dish. This is a more modern version, with the carrots tossed in harissa and fresh cilantro. It's fantastic served as a meze starter, with other salads, bread, and olives.

1. Put the carrots in a large pan of boiling water and cook for 7 to 8 minutes until just tender, but still with plenty of bite. Drain well.

2. Meanwhile, mash the garlic to a paste and add the cumin, paprika, harissa, red wine vinegar, and olive oil. Season and stir.

3. Put the warm cooked carrots in the bowl with the dressing and toss together. Leave to come to room temperature, mixing every few minutes. The carrots will soak up the flavors beautifully.

4. Once at room temperature, add the cilantro, stir, and serve.

Village Peppers

Serves 4
as a side

6 sweet green peppers

4 tablespoons olive oil

4 garlic cloves, roughly chopped

1 red chile

2 teaspoons paprika

Sea salt

This is such a simple salad, found in the villages strewn across the mountains of Morocco. It is made with charred sweet green peppers when there is a seasonal glut, cooked in a little olive oil, garlic, and spices. If you can't get the long, green peppers, use red Romano ones, not the green bell pepper variety, which is not sweet enough for this dish.

1. Cook the peppers on a hot grill or over a high gas flame for about 6 to 8 minutes until charred and tender. Put into a shallow dish and cover with plastic wrap. Leave to cool for about 5 minutes. Peel, discard the skin and stalk, and scrape off the seeds.

2. Heat the oil in a large frying pan over high heat. Add the garlic and chile and cook for a few seconds until fragrant. Add the peppers, paprika, and a pinch of salt. Toss together in the oil and serve immediately.

Forest Mushrooms

Serves 2

1 tablespoon butter

1 tablespoon olive oil

10 ounces mixed mushrooms, such as cremini and portobello, roughly sliced

3½ ounces chanterelle mushrooms

1 teaspoon dried oregano

2 garlic cloves, finely chopped

3 tomatoes, peeled and roughly chopped

2 tablespoons tomato purée

1 teaspoon ground cumin

½ teaspoon paprika, plus a pinch for garnish

A handful of finely chopped flat-leaf parsley leaves

2 slices of sourdough bread, toasted

1½ ounces firm goat cheese (log shape), sliced

Sea salt and freshly ground black pepper

In a tiny valley tucked away in the Rif Mountains, time has stood still for many years in the sleepy 300-year-old village of Ouled Ben Blida. It has about 40 houses, a tiny school, a soccer field, and some of the most spectacular views I have ever seen. On a beautifully sunny autumn afternoon, my hosts and I made our way into the surrounding Bouhachem Forest to forage for *fatar*, or wild mushrooms. It was a little early in the season, but we got lucky and managed to find enough to cook with. They were fried in butter, garlic, and tomatoes, with spices and wild herbs. The perfect brunch, I suggested, which was met with glares of dismay. This is a dinner dish, I learned, and not to be messed with. Regardless, it is delicious. The mellow mushrooms soak up all the other flavors, and a creamy goat cheese melts through them under the broiler.

1. Melt the butter with the oil in a large frying pan over high heat. Add the mixed mushrooms and season with salt and pepper. Toss together and leave for 4 to 5 minutes, shaking the pan occasionally, so that the mushrooms start to fry. Add the chanterelles, oregano, and garlic. Toss together, and cook for 3 to 4 minutes, shaking the pan occasionally, until golden.

2. Put the tomatoes, tomato purée, cumin, paprika, parsley, and 4 tablespoons of water into the pan. Mix well and stir-fry for 3 to 4 minutes, or until the tomatoes have broken down. Check the seasoning and remove from the heat.

3. Meanwhile, heat the broiler to high and place the toast on a baking sheet. Top the toast with the mushrooms and a few slices of goat cheese. Broil for 2 to 3 minutes to melt the cheese until oozy. Sprinkle with a pinch of paprika and serve immediately.

Vegetable Briwat

Makes 12

3½ ounces vermicelli noodles

2 tablespoons vegetable oil, plus extra for brushing the pastry

2 garlic cloves, finely chopped

1 carrot, grated

1 zucchini, grated and the excess moisture squeezed out

6 ounces white cabbage, finely sliced

½ red onion, finely chopped

5 ounces mushrooms, sliced

1 teaspoon ground ginger

1½ teaspoons ground cumin

1¼ teaspoons paprika

½ teaspoon ras el hanout (see note on page 180)

1 tablespoon butter

2 tablespoons all-purpose flour

6 sheets phyllo pastry

Sea salt and freshly ground black pepper

Briwat are deep-fried, stuffed filo pastry triangles. The sweet variety, often prepared during Ramadan, is filled with an almond mix and soaked in sugar syrup. Savory varieties contain a mix of veggies, sometimes with chicken or shrimp. They are the perfect appetizers.

1. Put the noodles into a mixing bowl and pour over enough just-boiled water to cover. Cover with plastic wrap and leave to soak for about 10 minutes. Drain well and put into a large mixing bowl. Cut the noodles with a pair of scissors to help them mix.

2. Heat the oil in a large wok over high heat. Add the garlic and stir-fry for few seconds, then add the other vegetables. Season well and stir-fry for 8 to 10 minutes, or until golden. Add all the spices and the butter and mix well. Add the vegetable mixture to the bowl with the noodles and mix well. Set aside to cool.

3. Preheat the oven to 400°F and mix the flour with 4 tablespoons of water to form a paste. Set aside. Check the seasoning of the cooled mix.

4. Cut one of the pieces of pastry in half lengthwise, so you have two long rectangles. Place one of them on a clean wooden board in a landscape orientation. Brush some of the flour paste around the edges—this will help to seal the pastries. Place a small portion of the mix (about the size of a large marble) in the center of the left half, a few inches from the left-hand side. Fold the bottom left edge over the mix to form a triangle shape. Push the top down to seal the side, and press the horizontal edge down tightly next to the mix. Then fold the pastry to the right, lifting the mix within the triangle shape you have created. Fold again, following the triangle shape, this time down towards you. Lift and fold over again, sealing the triangle. Brush the excess pastry (you can trim it if there is too much) with the flour paste and fold it over the top of the *briwat*, gently pressing it together. You should have a neat triangle shape. Place, fold side down, on a baking sheet lined with parchment paper. Repeat with the remaining pastry and filling. Brush the top of the *briwat* with a little oil and add a pinch of sea salt. Bake for 25 to 30 minutes until golden. Remove from the oven and leave to cool for 5 minutes or so, before serving.

Bakoula-style Spinach

Serves 4
as a side

1¼ pounds spinach

4 tablespoons olive oil

4 garlic cloves, crushed

A large handful of finely chopped cilantro leaves

A large handful of finely chopped flat-leaf parsley leaves

1 teaspoon ground cumin

1 teaspoon paprika

2 teaspoons harissa (page 183)

Juice of ½ lemon

Sea salt

Bakoula, or mallow, is a wide leafy green that grows wild in Morocco during the winter months. Bunches of the bitter leaves are finely chopped and stewed until soft, which mellows the flavor so that it's not unlike spinach. The wilted leaves are fried with herbs and spices and sometimes a little harissa for a kick. It's fantastic as a side dish with any tagine or a juicy grilled kebab, or as part of a cold meze. Mallow is hard to get hold of outside North Africa, so this is my spinach-based tribute to the traditional dish.

1. Wilt the spinach in a large pan for 2 to 3 minutes over medium heat with a tablespoon of water. Put into a colander and squeeze out any excess moisture with the back of a spoon. Finely chop.

2. Heat the oil in a frying pan over medium heat and add the garlic. Cook for 1 minute until golden, and then add the herbs, spices, and harissa. Mix together well.

3. Put the spinach in the pan and cook, stirring continuously, for 2 to 3 minutes to heat through. Add the lemon juice and a pinch of salt. Mix well and serve immediately.

Tomato & Garlic Sauce

Serves 4
as a side

2 (14-ounce) cans chopped tomatoes

2 tablespoons olive oil

4 garlic cloves, finely chopped

1 teaspoon ground cumin

1 teaspoon paprika

Sea salt

This rich tomato garlic sauce is delicious served with the seafood *bastillas* on page 110.

1. Put the tomatoes in a sieve and drain off the excess liquid.

2. Heat the oil in small pan over medium heat. Add the garlic and cook for 30 seconds until fragrant. Put in the tomatoes, and add the spices and a good pinch of salt. Mix well, reduce the heat to low and cook, stirring occasionally, for 8 to 10 minutes or until nice and thick. Serve.

Meat & Poultry

D'jaj m'Hamer

Serves 4 to 6

FOR THE MARINADE

2 teaspoons ground cumin

1 teaspoon ground black pepper

2 teaspoons paprika

½ teaspoon ground turmeric

2 teaspoons ground ginger

1 teaspoon ground cinnamon

A pinch of saffron

Zest and juice of 1 lemon

8 garlic cloves, roughly chopped

A small handful of roughly
chopped cilantro leaves

A small handful of roughly
chopped flat-leaf parsley leaves

4 tablespoons olive oil

Sea salt

1 free-range chicken, about 3
pounds, spatchcocked*

2 tablespoons olive oil

2 red onions, finely chopped

7 ounces chicken livers, finely
chopped to a pulp

1½ cups pitted green olives

2 preserved lemons (page 184),
seeds scraped out and the rest
finely chopped

2 tablespoons butter

A small handful of finely
chopped flat-leaf parsley leaves

Lemon wedges, green salad
and French fries, to serve

*to spatchcock your chicken, place it
breast-side down on a chopping board.
Use a really strong pair of scissors to
cut it, either side of the spine, from the
neck to the tail, cutting through the rib
bones as you go. Remove the spine and
discard. Now pull apart the chicken and
open it out. Turn it over and push down
onto the breastbone with the heel of
your hand to flatten the chicken out.*

Translated as "red chicken," a reference to the bird's being poached in spices and then fried until crisp (reddish), this is a knock-out Moroccan meal. I had seen fried chicken and French fries on a few menus and slightly turned my nose up at it. However, once I tried the real deal, I was hooked. The meat soaks up all the flavor of the aromatic herbs and spices, and is then cooked again to turn golden. I favor the broiler rather than frying—I just find it easier. The sauce is then reduced until rich and thick. Whip up a batch of homemade fries or have a root around the freezer to see if you have any lurking at the back.

1. Put all the ingredients for the marinade into a spice grinder. Season well and blend to a smooth paste. Cut a few slits into the legs of the chicken and place in a shallow dish. Rub the paste all over, making sure that the whole bird is completely covered. Push the marinade under the skin. Cover and marinate overnight.

2. Heat the oil in a large, lidded shallow pan over medium heat. Add the onions and cook, stirring occasionally, for 5 to 6 minutes. Add the chicken livers, olives, and preserved lemons, and cook, stirring, for 30 seconds. Place the chicken, breast-side down, into the pan and pour over enough water to cover by about two-thirds (about 2⅔ cups). Bring to a boil over high heat. Cover, reduce the heat to low, and cook for 1½ hours, or until the chicken is cooked through and beautifully juicy. If the lid doesn't quite close, weight it down with something heavy to reduce evaporation.

3. Preheat the broiler to high. Remove the chicken from the sauce and place on a baking sheet. Rub the butter over the top and place under the hot broiler for 10 minutes to become golden and crispy. Remove from the broiler and place in a warm serving dish. Cover with foil and leave to rest for 10 minutes.

4. Meanwhile, bring the pan back to a boil over medium-high heat and cook, stirring occasionally, for 15 to 20 minutes. Spoon some of the juices over the chicken and serve the remainder in a ramekin. Scatter over the parsley and serve immediately with lemon wedges and a green salad. Oh, and don't forget the fries!

Chicken & Date Pilaf

Serves 4

2 tablespoons olive oil

1½ pounds chicken thighs on the bone

2 red onions, finely sliced

3 tomatoes, finely chopped

2½ cups chicken stock

5 dates, pitted and roughly chopped

¼ teaspoon ground cinnamon

1 teaspoon *baharat*

1½ teaspoons paprika

1½ cups basmati rice

5 ounces Greek yogurt

2 tablespoons harissa (page 183)

Cumin salt (page 180), to serve

A small handful of finely chopped flat-leaf parsley leaves

3 tablespoons toasted almonds

Sea salt and freshly ground black pepper

My fragrant pilaf is such a simple dish, flavored with aromatic *baharat*—an Arabic spice mix, made with paprika, pepper, cloves, and cinnamon—and served with a harissa yogurt. It's not typically Moroccan, but uses all the flavors, mixing sweet dates with a savory, spiced rice. It cooks in one dish, with all the lovely aromas mingling together. Perfect to feed a crowd.

1. Heat the oil in a large pan over medium heat. Add the chicken, skin-side down, and brown for 6 to 8 minutes. Remove from the pan and set aside.

2. Put the onions into the hot pan, mix well, and cook for 2 to 3 minutes to soften—they may need a little longer. Add the tomatoes and season well. Mix everything together, scraping the nice sticky bits off the base of the pan, and cook for 4 to 5 minutes so that the tomatoes break down.

3. Pour in the stock, then add the dates, cinnamon, *baharat,* and paprika. Bring to a boil and add the rice. Mix once and return the chicken to the pan. Cover, reduce the heat to low, and cook for 35 to 40 minutes, or until the rice is tender and the chicken cooked through. Remove from the heat and take off the lid. Cover with a clean dish towel and put the lid back on. Leave for 5 minutes so that the rice can fluff up.

4. Meanwhile, mix the yogurt and harissa together in a bowl with a pinch of salt.

5. Season the rice with cumin salt and scatter over the parsley and almonds. Serve immediately with the harissa yogurt.

Rfissa

Serves 4

3 tablespoons olive oil

2 pounds chicken thighs on the bone

2 red onions, sliced

6 garlic cloves, roughly sliced

2 tomatoes, finely chopped

2 tablespoons tomato purée

2 teaspoons ground ginger

2 teaspoons ras el hanout (see note on page 180)

1 teaspoon ground black pepper

A pinch of saffron threads

4 cups chicken stock

½ cup green lentils

½ cup split peas, soaked overnight

1 bunch of roughly chopped cilantro leaves

2 tablespoons butter

2 free-range eggs

8 small chapati flatbreads

Sea salt

This dish, also known as *trid*, is a celebratory meal, prepared especially for the birth of a baby. The chicken is flavored with plenty of ras el hanout, saffron, and ginger and cooked with lentils and split peas, creating a rich stew. The correct way to serve *rfissa* is in a large dish, strewn with shredded pieces of freshly prepared *msemen*, a flaky bread, which soaks up all the sauce. You can find a stuffed version of this bread on page 16. Don't judge, but to save time I use store-bought flatbread, which I cut into strips and use as the base instead.

1. Heat the oil in a heavy-based casserole over high heat and cook the chicken for 3 to 4 minutes each side until golden. Remove from the pan and set aside.

2. Reheat the pan over medium heat and add the onions and garlic. Cook, stirring occasionally, for 6 to 8 minutes until golden. Add the tomatoes and tomato purée. Mix well and cook for 1 to 2 minutes or until the tomatoes start to break down.

3. Add the ginger, ras el hanout, pepper, saffron, and a good pinch of salt. Mix well and return the chicken to the pan. Pour in the stock and add lentils, split peas, and half the cilantro. Mix everything together really well. Bring to a boil, cover, reduce the heat to low and cook for 2 to 2½ hours, or until the chicken is cooked through and the split peas are really soft and tender. Once cooked, add the butter and most of the remaining cilantro. Mix together so the butter melts and makes the sauce glossy.

4. Meanwhile, bring a pan of water to a boil and hard-boil the eggs for 6 to 8 minutes. Drain, peel, and chop into quarters.

5. Heat a non-stick frying pan over high heat. Cook the chapatis for 10 to 20 seconds each side to get a little color. Slice into strips and put in a large serving dish. Top with the cooked chicken and spoon over the pulses and wonderful sauce. Arrange the eggs over the top and scatter over the remaining cilantro. Serve immediately.

Tfaya with Moroccan Sauté

Serves 4

FOR THE CHICKEN

1¼ pounds chicken thighs, roughly sliced

Juice of ½ lemon

2 tablespoons olive oil

3 garlic cloves

2 tomatoes, finely chopped

1 tablespoon tomato purée

1 (14-ounce) can chickpeas, rinsed and drained

1 teaspoon ground ginger

1 teaspoon dry chermoula (page 180)

½ teaspoon ground cumin

1 small bunch of finely chopped flat-leaf parsley leaves, to serve

Sea salt and freshly ground black pepper

FOR THE *TFAYA*

1½ tablespoons butter

2 red onions, finely sliced

¼ teaspoon ground ginger

¼ teaspoon ground cinnamon

A pinch of ground turmeric

A pinch of ground black pepper

A pinch of sugar

3 tablespoons raisins, soaked in water for about 5 minutes

1 teaspoon lemon juice

Made with caramelized onions, raisins, cinnamon, and sugar, *tfaya* is the sweet slick that gives a decadent finish to savory dishes, from tagines to couscous. It's the cherry on top, to lux out the meal for a special occasion—like the Seven Vegetables Couscous on page 50. Catering for the Moroccan sweet tooth, it should have bucket loads of sugar, but my palate (and my dentist) are not so keen. So my version omits all but a pinch of sugar, as I feel the sweetness of the onions is enough. I serve *tfaya* with a really simple sautéed chicken in sauce, flavored with dry chermoula and cumin.

1. Put the chicken thighs in a shallow dish, pour over the lemon juice, and season with salt. Mix together. Cover and refrigerate overnight to marinate and tenderize.

2. Take the chicken out of the fridge to come to room temperature. Heat the oil and garlic in a large frying pan over high heat. Add the chicken and stir-fry for 10 to 12 minutes. Be patient: lots of moisture will come out of the meat before it starts to brown. Once the liquid evaporates, the thighs will fry and turn gloriously golden.

3. Add the tomatoes, tomato purée, chickpeas, ginger, chermoula, cumin, and a good pinch of salt and pepper to the pan. Pour over ½ cup of just-boiled water and mix well. Cook for 2 to 3 minutes until you have a thick sauce. Remove from the heat, cover the pan and steam for 3 to 4 minutes to soften the chickpeas.

4. Meanwhile, make the *tfaya*. Melt the butter in a small frying pan over medium heat. Add the onions and a pinch of salt. Cook, stirring occasionally, for 10 to 12 minutes until golden and sticky. Add the ginger, cinnamon, turmeric, pepper, and sugar. Add the drained raisins, 3 tablespoons of water, and the lemon juice. Mix until thick then remove from the heat.

5. Scatter the parsley over the cooked chicken and serve immediately with the *tfaya* spooned over the top.

Seffa

Serves 4

4 tablespoons olive oil

8 chicken thighs (about 2 pounds), skin and bone on

1 red onion, finely chopped

2 garlic cloves, crushed

5 ounces chicken livers, finely chopped

1 tomato, finely chopped

A chicken stock cube

A pinch of saffron threads

2 tablespoons tomato purée

2 teaspoons ras el hanout (see note on page 180)

1 teaspoon ground ginger

1 teaspoon ground black pepper

2 tablespoons butter

A handful of finely chopped flat-leaf parsley leaves

10 ounces vermicelli noodles

¼ cup sliced almonds

A pinch of ground cinnamon

Sea salt

Another celebratory dish, this wonderfully tender chicken is served with vermicelli noodles, a saffron-fragrant sauce, and loads of almonds. This really is the ultimate home-cooked food. And I learned it from the best—Naima and her friend Hasna, a Saharaoui from a Saharan tribe in the deep south of Morocco.

1. Heat half the oil in a heavy-bottomed Dutch oven over medium heat. Add the chicken, skin-side down, and brown all over for 8 to 10 minutes. Remove from the pan and set aside. Put the onion in the pan and cook, stirring occasionally, for 3 to 4 minutes until translucent. Add the garlic, livers, and tomato, and cook for about a minute until you can smell the sweet garlic.

2. Meanwhile, put the stock cube into a heatproof measuring cup and pour over 2 cups of just-boiled water. Add the saffron and whisk together. Leave for a few minutes to infuse. The saffron will bleed its deep orange color into the stock.

3. Pour the stock into the pan and add the tomato purée, ras el hanout, ginger, pepper, and a small pinch of salt. Mix well and bring to a boil. Return the chicken to the pan, skin-side up, cover, and reduce the heat to low. Simmer gently for 45 minutes to 1 hour, or until the chicken is cooked and tender. Remove the chicken from the pan and set aside.

4. Add the butter to the sauce and mix well. Turn up the heat and bubble gently for 8 to 10 minutes or until the sauce has reduced by half. Check the seasoning, and return the chicken to the pan. Add most of the parsley and mix well.

5. Meanwhile, cook the noodles according to the packet instructions in a pot of boiling water. Once cooked, drain and return to the pan. Drizzle over the remaining 2 tablespoons of olive oil and toss together.

6. To serve the dish, divide the noodles between four serving bowls. Top each one with chicken and spoon over some of the juices. Garnish with the remaining parsley, almonds, and a light dusting of cinnamon. Serve immediately with any remaining juices in a bowl on the table.

Aicha's Chicken Couscous

Serves 4 to 6

3 tablespoons olive oil

4 full chicken legs (e.g. legs and thighs, not just drumsticks)

1 red onion, finely chopped

2 garlic cloves, sliced

2 tomatoes, roughly chopped

4 tablespoons tomato purée

A small pinch of saffron threads

2 teaspoons paprika

2 teaspoons ground cumin

1 teaspoon ground turmeric

1 teaspoon ground ginger

A handful of finely chopped cilantro leaves and stems, plus extra to garnish

1²/₃ cups chicken stock

12 ounces baby eggplants, slit down the middle

3 green chiles, skins pricked with a sharp knife

½ cup pitted black olives

1 cup plus 2 tablespooons couscous

3 tablespoons sliced almonds

Sea salt and freshly ground black pepper

This superb Berber dish is a celebratory meal, served at weddings and on other religious occasions. I was fortunate enough to be invited to a pre-wedding dinner in the little village of Ouled Ben Blida, where my friend Muhammed's daughter was getting married. His wife, Aicha, cooked this wonderful couscous, served with freshly baked bread from their outdoor, wood-fired oven. For the wedding they had brought in extra couscous, fizzy drinks, and flour to make bread; they were expecting more than a hundred guests from the local tribes. Here's my take on Aicha's beautiful chicken dish.

1. Heat the oil in a large, shallow pan over medium heat. Add the chicken pieces and brown for 3 to 4 minutes each side. Remove from the pan and set aside.

2. Add the onion to the pan and cook, stirring occasionally, for 3 to 4 minutes until soft. Throw in the garlic and cook for 10 seconds until fragrant, then add the tomatoes and mix well. Cook, stirring occasionally, for 2 to 3 minutes so the tomatoes break down, then add the tomato purée, spices, and cilantro. Season with salt and pepper, pour in the stock, and mix well.

3. Return the chicken to the pan, and put the eggplants and chiles on top. Bring to a boil, cover, reduce the heat to low, and cook for 45 minutes to 1 hour, or until the chicken is cooked and the eggplants soft.

4. Remove the lid and increase the heat slightly so the sauce starts to bubble away. Add the olives and cook, stirring occasionally, for 10 to 15 minutes until the sauce reduces a little.

5. Meanwhile, put the couscous in a bowl. Season with salt and pepper, and pour over enough just-boiled water to cover by about ¼ inch. Cover with plastic wrap and set aside until the water has been absorbed. Fluff up with a fork once ready.

6. Scatter the extra cilantro and almonds over the cooked chicken and serve immediately with the couscous.

Chermoula Spiced Chicken

Serves 6

1 free-range chicken, about 3 pounds

1 quantity of chermoula paste (page 183)

1½ tablespoons butter

1 teaspoon ras el hanout (see note on page 180)

2 preserved lemons (page 184)

Sea salt

This was cooked for me in the beautiful blue town of Chefchaouen by Fouad, a local chef who owns a restaurant in the heart of the medina. He marinated the chicken in spices and boiled it until tender. Once cooked, he put it into a shallow dish and took it to the communal baker (which was conveniently next to his restaurant) and got the baker to roast the bird in the wood-fired oven until golden and crispy. Sadly I don't have a communal bakery at my disposal, so I have adapted the recipe to work in my oven. It is utterly divine, and great served with bread, a tomato and onion salad (see page 43), and plenty of mayonnaise.

1. Place the chicken in a large mixing bowl. Make a deep slash in both legs and prick the underside all over with a knife. Pour over half the chermoula, and rub it all over the bird, inside and out, and under the skin. Cover and leave to marinate in the fridge overnight.

2. Preheat the oven to 425°F and take the chicken out of the fridge to come to room temperature. Melt the butter, ras el hanout, and a pinch of salt together for 20 seconds in a microwave.

3. Place the chicken in an oiled roasting pan and spread the remaining chermoula marinade over it. Stuff the preserved lemons into the cavity of the bird and brush the top with the melted butter. Place in the hot oven and cook for 1 hour 10 minutes to 1½ hours, or until the juices run clear. Remove from the oven and baste the chicken really well. Cover with foil and leave to rest for 15 minutes. Carve up and serve with the juices spooned over the top, and the remaining chermoula in a bowl at the table.

Pulled Lamb Méchoui

Serves 4

3 garlic cloves, peeled
2 tablespoons butter
2 teaspoons ras el-hanout
(see note on page 180)
1 teaspoon ground cumin
1 teaspoon ground coriander
2 teaspoons olive oil
3 pounds lamb shoulder, skinless
(weight includes bone)
A handful of roughly chopped
flat-leaf parsley leaves
A handful of roughly chopped
mint leaves
1½ ounces feta cheese
¾ cup pomegranate seeds
Sea salt

Méchoui is a very traditional Berber lamb barbecue dish. To learn about it, I traveled deep into the High Atlas Mountains with my friend Lachen. A huge fire pit was prepared, made of mud in a cone shape. We tied the lamb carcass to a wooden cross and rubbed *smen* (fermented butter) all over it. Then we lowered the cross into the pit so that the lamb was suspended over the fire, before sealing the top of the makeshift oven with more mud. Then we waited, enjoying the stunning scenery, and eating *boulfaf* (page 85). When the lamb was ready, we broke the seal and lifted it out. The meat was served on a bed of wild herbs, with bread and spices to season. We ate with our fingers, ripping off pieces of meat, juicy and crisp. To do this at home would be quite a project, I admit, but a slow-roasted lamb shoulder works just as well. And to lighten up the rich flavors, a final showering of fresh herbs, salty feta, and pomegranate seeds adds an incredible finish. (Pictured overleaf.)

1. Using a mortar and pestle, grind the garlic to a paste with a little salt. Add the butter, followed by the spices, olive oil, and a little more salt, mixing until smooth. Prick the lamb all over with the tip of a sharp knife and place in a large mixing bowl. Rub the spice paste all over the lamb. Cover and refrigerate overnight.

2. Preheat the oven to 425°F and take the lamb out of the fridge to come to room temperature. Place in a roasting pan and pour a scant ½ cup of water around the sides. Cover with foil and put into the hot oven. Reduce the heat to 400°F and cook for 3 hours or until the meat is tender and can be pulled apart with a fork. Remove from the oven, cover, and leave to rest for 20 minutes.

3. Using two forks shred the lamb. Transfer to a serving plate, season with salt, and mix together. Scatter over the herbs and crumble over the feta. Finally add the pomegranate seeds and serve immediately.

Boulfaf

Serves 2
8 long skewers, soaked
in cold water if wooden

10 ounces lamb liver, cut
into ½-inch cubes

1½ ounces lamb fat, cut
into ¼-inch cubes

2 tablespoons olive oil

3 teaspoons ground cumin

3 teaspoons paprika

Sea salt and freshly ground
black pepper

We had just buried a lamb to roast in the ground for *méchoui* (page 81), and the meat's aroma was already wafting out, making me hungry. I was in the village of Tacheddirt in the High Atlas Mountains, population around 300, and they were not used to wandering chefs with a passion for smoke and fire, so we had a good turnout. I was sitting on a small terrace overlooking the stunning scenery on a fresh October afternoon. My hosts were drinking mint tea, and I was wondering how long it would be until the food was ready. Then I noticed a small barbecue being set up. Long kebabs threaded with liver and lamb fat were seasoned with masses of cumin, pepper, and salt, and grilled for a few minutes on the hot coals. This was *boulfaf*, traditionally eaten before the roasted lamb *méchoui*. As they cooked, the melting lamb fat kept the liver beautifully moist. To prepare these kebabs the fat is a must; it is what keeps them so juicy, so do ask your butcher for some. You won't be disappointed.

1. Preheat the barbecue to high. Thread the meat and fat onto skewers, alternating between the two. Line the skewers up on a chopping board and drizzle over the oil. Twist them around so they get completely coated, and season well with salt.

2. Cook over the hot barbecue for 4 to 8 minutes in total, turning every 30 seconds, or when golden. Once beautifully crispy, but with the liver still a little pink, transfer to a clean chopping board. Shower with cumin, paprika, and more salt. Serve immediately with bread, tea, and more seasoning.

M'Hamer Royal Lamb

Serves 4

3 tablespoons butter

2 tablespoons olive oil

2 onions, roughly chopped

6 garlic cloves, finely chopped

1½ pounds boneless lamb shoulder, cut into 3 to 4-inch pieces

2 teaspoons paprika, plus an extra pinch for the almonds

1 teaspoon ground ginger

¼ teaspoon ground turmeric

A pinch of saffron threads

4 cups lamb stock

¼ cup whole blanched almonds

Sea salt and freshly ground black pepper

The royal cities of Fez, Marrakesh, Meknes, and Rabat were responsible for honing the culinary traditions of Morocco and developing lavish dishes for the monarchs and their guests. This intense red, paprika-flavored lamb is one of the best, and, according to several chefs I spoke to, originates from Fez. The meat is cooked slowly with paprika, ground ginger, and saffron, infusing with their aromas. Once cooked, the lamb falls apart at the touch of a fork, and the sauce is reduced until deeply savory and rich. The finished dish is adorned with almonds, which I like to toast with more paprika, for a decadent finish.

1. Melt 2 tablespoons of the butter with the oil in a large pan over medium heat. Add the onions and cook, stirring occasionally, for 8 to 10 minutes until golden. Add the garlic, mix well, and cook for 10 seconds until fragrant.

2. Put the meat into the pan and add the paprika, ginger, turmeric, saffron, stock, and a good pinch of salt and pepper. Mix everything together really well. Bring to a boil, cover, reduce the heat to low and cook for 2 to 2½ hours, or until the meat is beautifully tender. It should literally fall apart if you poke it with a fork. Using a slotted spoon, transfer the meat to a warm dish. Cover with foil and set aside to rest.

3. Reheat the sauce over high heat until boiling. Reduce to medium and cook for 20 to 25 minutes, stirring occasionally, until really rich and thick. Skim off the fat as it rises to the surface.

4. Meanwhile, heat a small frying pan over medium heat and add the almonds. Toast for 8 to 10 minutes, shaking the pan occasionally, or until the nuts are golden on all sides. Remove from the heat and add the remaining butter. Swirl together around the pan until melted. Add a pinch of paprika and salt. Toss together and immediately transfer to a small plate to cool.

5. To serve, return the lamb to the pan and stir gently to coat it in the intensified flavors of the sauce. Transfer to a serving dish, and scatter with the cooked almonds. Serve immediately.

Berber Medfouna

Serves 6 to 8

FOR THE DOUGH

2 cups all-purpose flour

2 tablespoons olive oil

1 teaspoon (half a packet) active dry yeast

¾ to 1 cup warm water

Sea salt

FOR THE FILLING

3 tablespoons olive oil, plus extra for drizzling

7 ounces lamb leg, with plenty of fat, cut into small cubes

1 onion, finely chopped

1 carrot, grated

1 zucchini, grated and the excess moisture squeezed out

A handful of finely chopped chives

A handful of finely chopped flat-leaf parsley leaves

2 teaspoons paprika

2 teaspoons harissa (page 183), plus extra to serve

Sea salt and freshly ground black pepper

Deep in the desert of Skoura, in the south of Morocco, I was cooked this delicious dish by Aicha, a fabulous Berber woman, with traditional tattoos and vibrant clothing. She cooked with such skill, and it was a pleasure to watch as she rolled out the dough and stuffed it with the lamb mix, which was spiked with little chunks of fried fat for extra flavor.

1. Sift the flour into a shallow mixing bowl, add the olive oil and a good pinch of sea salt. Make a well in the center and add the yeast. Pour about ¼ cup of water over the yeast and leave for a few minutes to activate. Then slowly add the rest of the water, mixing as you go with your hands. Add more water if the dough seems too dry or flour if it's too wet. Turn onto a floured surface and knead for about 10 minutes until smooth. Place in an oiled mixing bowl, cover, and leave to rise for about 30 minutes.

2. Heat 1 tablespoon of the oil in a frying pan over medium-high heat. Add the lamb and stir-fry for 4 to 5 minutes until golden. Add the onion and stir-fry for a further 1 to 2 minutes.

3. Remove the lamb from the pan and finely chop. Put into a mixing bowl along with the cooked onions. Add the remaining filling ingredients and mix everything together really well.

4. Divide the dough in half and roll into balls. On a floured board, use the palm of your hand to press one of the balls into a flat circle. Take half of the lamb mix and place in the center of the dough. Pull the top edge of the dough up and about half way over the mix. Continue doing this around the circle of dough, pulling it up and over the mixture to close it. You can be quite firm, sticking the sides together in the middle as you go along. Once sealed, drizzle each side with a little oil and keep pressing until you have a 8-inch round pizza shape. Repeat with the other dough ball.

5. Heat 1 tablespoon oil in a large non-stick frying pan over medium-high heat. Place one *medfouna*, seal-side down, in the pan. This is the thinner side so it needs less cooking. Reduce the heat to medium-low and cook for 3 to 4 minutes until golden. Flip and cook the thicker side for 4 to 6 minutes until the dough is cooked. Transfer to a warm serving dish and cover. Repeat with the other *medfouna*. Rest for 5 minutes before serving with harissa.

My Bazaar Burger

Serves 4

1 garlic clove

1¼ teaspoons paprika

¾ teaspoon ras el hanout
(see note on page 180)

1¼ teaspoons ground cumin

1 pound ground lamb (try for
20% fat)

1 eggplant

1 teaspoon harissa (page 183)

3 tablespoons mayonnaise

4 brioche buns, halved

1 onion, thinly sliced

Juice of ½ lemon

2 tablespoons olive oil

4 slices of hard cheese,
such as cheddar or Gruyère

Baby gem lettuce

Sea salt and freshly ground
black pepper

High on the rooftops above Marrakesh, Nomad restaurant serves up wonderful modern Moroccan food. The views are spectacular. You can soak up the souk experience as you dine, and they do a mean burger. This is my version, well spiced with classic seasonings and served with a luscious layer of smoked eggplant mayonnaise. Once cooked, I steam my burgers for a few seconds with the cheese and bun on top. The cheese melts and the bun fluffs up, giving you a really incredible texture.

1. Mash the garlic with a little salt. Mix the paprika, ras el hanout, ¾ teaspoon of the cumin, and a good pinch of pepper in a small bowl. Place the lamb in a mixing bowl and add the garlic and most of the spices, setting some aside. Mix well. Cover and marinate in the fridge for at least an hour or overnight.

2. Prick the eggplant all over with a fork and roast over a high gas flame for about 10 to 12 minutes, turning regularly, until soft and charred. (Alternatively, roast the eggplant in a 500°F oven until collapsed.) Set aside to cool, then peel. Discard the skin and finely chop the flesh. Turn into a large bowl and mix in the harissa, mayonnaise, a good pinch of salt, and the remaining cumin.

3. Heat a griddle pan over high heat and toast the brioche bottoms for 20 to 30 seconds on the cut side to char.

4. Mix the onion with the lemon juice and a pinch of salt. Leave for 5 minutes to soften.

5. Form the meat into four burgers. Heat the oil in a frying pan over medium-high heat. Season the outside of the burgers with the remaining spice mix and a pinch of salt. Cook the burgers for 4 to 6 minutes each side, flipping them every 2 minutes, until they are just cooked and nicely juicy.

6. Top the burgers with the cheese and brioche top buns. Add a tablespoon of water to the side of the pan to create some steam. Cover and leave for a few seconds. To serve, dollop a good amount of the eggplant paste onto the bottom burger buns. Cover with a few lettuce leaves and some of the onion slices. Top with the burgers and soft top buns. The cheese should be oozing everywhere. Serve immediately.

Lamb & Orzo Chorba

Serves 4

2 tablespoons olive oil

1 onion, finely chopped

2 garlic cloves, roughly sliced

8 ounces ground lamb

1 teaspoon *baharat* or dry chermoula (page 180)

1 teaspoon paprika

1 (14-ounce) can chopped tomatoes

2 tablespoons tomato purée

A small handful of finely chopped flat-leaf parsley leaves

A small handful of finely chopped cilantro leaves

4 cups lamb stock

¼ cup orzo

1½ tablespoons butter

1 tablespoon flour

Sea salt and freshly ground black pepper

Chorba is a really lovely, thick soup packed with veggies, chickpeas, pasta, and sometimes meat—it could be considered Morocco's answer to minestrone. It's hearty and thick, great for keeping shepherds (or lively little ones) full all afternoon. Originally an Ottoman soup that arrived via Algeria, it's the perfect tonic on a cold night. I have done a really quick version using ground lamb and orzo, a tiny pasta shape that's perfect for soup. Feel free to add in any vegetables you want, allowing enough time for them to soften; carrots, zucchini, and celery all work well. To mix it up, I sometimes make the soup without the meat, blend it, and then cook it with tiny lamb meatballs. Either way, it's fantastic.

1. Heat the oil in a pan over medium heat and add the onion. Cook, stirring occasionally, for 4 to 5 minutes until soft. Add the garlic and cook for 10 seconds until fragrant, then add the lamb. Stir-fry for 2 to 3 minutes to break up and start the cooking process.

2. Add in the spices, season well, and add the tomatoes, tomato purée, herbs, and the stock. Bring to a boil and add the orzo. Cover, reduce the heat to low, and simmer for 30 minutes until the orzo is cooked through.

3. Meanwhile, make a roux by mixing the butter with the flour in a small bowl until smooth.

4. Using a hand-held stick blender, give the soup a blast to help thicken it. I like mine with some texture. Stir in the roux, cover, and simmer for a further 10 minutes, stirring occasionally, to cook the flour. If the soup looks too thick, add a little water to loosen. Check the seasoning and serve immediately.

Lubia Belkarah

Serves 4

10 ounces dried cannellini beans

4 tablespoons olive oil

4 lamb shanks (about 14 ounces each)

3 red onions, finely chopped

5 garlic cloves, finely chopped

2 large tomatoes, roughly chopped

2 tablespoons tomato purée

2 teaspoons ground cumin

2 teaspoons ground ginger

1 teaspoon ground turmeric

A small pinch of saffron threads

6 cups lamb stock

1 lemon

A handful of finely chopped flat-leaf parsley leaves

Harissa (page 183), to serve

Sea salt

As part of my research for this book, I stayed with a Berber cook in the desert near the town of Ouarzazate, the gateway to the Sahara. It was a fascinating experience. I ate food I had never even heard of before. It was the end of the summer and the warm days were perfect for salads, soups, and fruit. But I wanted to learn to cook something heartier, so I asked my hosts for a classic winter dish. I was swiftly presented with a cow's leg, skin and all, and a hacksaw. Interesting. We burned off the skin, sawed the leg in half, and stewed the pieces for hours with white beans and spices. This was food to sustain the shepherds during the cold winter months: substantial, full of energy and fat, and bloody good. Now, you're not going to find a whole cow's leg in the aisle of your local supermarket, so I have adapted the recipe using lamb shanks. They work brilliantly.

1. Soak the beans in a pan of water overnight. Drain and set aside.

2. Heat the oil in a large pan over high heat and brown the lamb shanks on all sides—allow about 8 to 10 minutes. Remove from the pan and set aside.

3. Reduce the heat to medium and add the onions to the pan. Cook, stirring occasionally, for 4 to 5 minutes, and then add the garlic. Mix for a few seconds—the pan will be really hot, so make sure it does not burn—and then add the tomatoes, tomato purée, spices, and a small pinch of salt. Mix together into a thick paste. Pour in the stock and mix well.

4. Add the beans to the pan, and nestle the lamb shanks into the stock. Bring to a boil, cover, reduce the heat to low, and cook for about 2 hours until the beans are tender. Remove the lid and cook for a further 1 to 1½ hours, or until the sauce is really thick.

5. Squeeze in the juice of half the lemon to cut through the richness, and add the parsley. Mix well. At this point check the seasoning; it may well need more salt. Serve immediately with the remaining half lemon cut into wedges and plenty of harissa.

Truck Stop Kefta

Serves 2
as a main or
4 as part of a meal

FOR THE SAUCE

2 tablespoons olive oil

1 red onion, finely chopped

3 garlic cloves, crushed

5 tomatoes, seeds squeezed out, and flesh roughly chopped

2 tablespoons tomato purée

½ teaspoon ground ginger

½ teaspoon paprika, plus a pinch for seasoning

½ teaspoon ground cumin

2/3 cup just-boiled water

2 free-range eggs

A small handful of finely chopped flat-leaf parsley leaves

Moroccan bread or my Batbout Breakfast Bread (page 30), to serve

Sea salt and freshly ground black pepper

FOR THE MEATBALLS

10 ounces ground beef

1 garlic clove, crushed

¼ teaspoon paprika

¼ teaspoon ground cumin

A small handful of finely chopped flat-leaf parsley leaves

Whenever I travel I'm always looking for the best places to eat. Mostly that's in people's homes. But, as is often the case, it's not always possible to have a magnificent home-cooked meal rustled up for you at the click of your fingers. Boo! On a recent trip to Morocco, everyone kept telling me to eat at the service stations if I was in need of a bite to eat. Because I live in London, to me, service station food doesn't exactly mean gourmet. However, after being advised for the third time to eat at the local gas station I went, and got a real surprise. Forget overpriced sandwiches and stale coffee—in Morocco, service stations are where you get home-style food, cooked quick. Now I'm in the know, my gas station go-to is always beef *kefta*; little meatballs cooked in a tomato sauce with egg. It's fantastic, and a real taste of a mid-week meal, Morocco style.

1. To make the sauce, heat the oil in a large frying pan over medium heat. Add the onion and cook, stirring occasionally, for 5 to 6 minutes until golden. Add the garlic and cook for 10 seconds until fragrant. Add the tomatoes, tomato purée, spices, and a good pinch of salt. Pour in the just-boiled water and mix well. Cover, reduce the heat to low, and cook, stirring occasionally, for 15 minutes until rich and thick.

2. Meanwhile make the meatballs. Put the meat into a mixing bowl and add the garlic, spices, parsley, and good pinch of salt and pepper. Mix everything together really well. Using your hands, roll the mix into penny-sized meatballs.

3. Remove the lid from the pan and increase the heat to medium until the sauce is bubbling. Add the meatballs and shake the pan a little to help them sink in. Cook over low heat for 4 to 5 minutes, or until half cooked, then turn the meatballs. Make two wells in the sauce and crack in the eggs. Season with salt, pepper, and paprika. Cook for 4 to 6 minutes until the eggs have just set. Scatter over the parsley and serve immediately with bread.

Baharat Beef Rice

Serves 4

1½ cups basmati rice

2 tablespoons olive oil

1 onion, finely chopped

4 garlic cloves, finely chopped

4 tomatoes, finely chopped

2 tablespoons tomato purée

2 teaspoons paprika

2 teaspoons ground cumin

½ teaspoon ground black pepper

½ teaspoon baharat

10 ounces ground beef

2½ cups beef stock

A handful of finely chopped flat-leaf parsley leaves

2 tablespoons sliced almonds, to serve

Sea salt

Rice is not hugely popular in Morocco—they tend to favor bread or couscous—but you do find the odd dish, including a cold rice meze salad and this *baharat* beef rice, which I ate for the first time in the Atlas Mountains. My friend Lachen cooked it for me. We sat on the flat roof of his house, looking out onto the valley below Toubkal Mountain as we ate. The rice was cooked with spices and ground meat, and served as an accompaniment to grilled kebabs.

1. Wash the rice until the water runs clear, and drain thoroughly.

2. Heat the oil in a large pan over medium heat and add the onion. Cook, stirring occasionally, for 4 to 5 minutes, until a little golden. Add the garlic and cook for 10 seconds until fragrant. Add the tomatoes, tomato purée, spices, and beef, then season with salt. Mix well to break up the meat.

3. Turn the rice into the pan and mix well to coat the grains in oil. Pour over the stock and mix once. Bring to a boil, cover, reduce the heat to low and cook for 10 to 12 minutes, or until all the water is absorbed. Remove from the heat. Cover with a dish towel and leave for 10 minutes to fluff up.

4. Add half the parsley and fork into the rice. Check the seasoning and add more salt if required. Turn onto a serving plate and scatter over the almonds and remaining parsley. Serve immediately.

Seafood

Anchovies in Olive Oil & Tomato

Serves 2

4 tablespoons olive oil

2 garlic cloves, crushed

A handful of finely chopped flat-leaf parsley leaves

1½ teaspoons ground cumin

1 teaspoon paprika

1 cup tomato sauce

Juice of ½ lemon

8 to 10 small fresh anchovy fillets, washed and cleaned

Extra virgin olive oil, for drizzling

Crusty bread, to serve

Sea salt

From Tangier in the north to Saïda on the country's eastern border is Mediterranean Morocco, directly facing Spain. There is a long history between the two countries, and the region of Andalucía in particular has left an imprint on the food, music, textiles, and even the architecture of Morocco's northeast, in particular the town of Chefchaouen in the Rif Mountains. The town is famous for its blue painted buildings. Some stories go that this hue is a legacy of its Jewish settlers for whom the color was a reminder of their spiritual awareness, while others claim that it is to keep away mosquitoes, who apparently hate the color! This is one of the most extraordinary places in the world to visit. But Chefchaouen, with its wide squares, cobbled streets, tiled roofs, and wide, open windows, also feels different from other Moroccan towns. The food has a Spanish influence, and this simple dish is a twist on boquerónes—a favorite Spanish appetizer of marinated anchovies. Delicately spiced, these mouthwatering Moroccan morsels make a fantastic starter or addition to a meze meal.

1. Heat the oil in a large frying pan over medium-high heat. Add the garlic and cook for 10 seconds until fragrant. Add the parsley and spices and mix well. Working quickly, so that the spices don't burn, add the tomato sauce, lemon juice, and a good pinch of salt. Mix well and cook, stirring occasionally, for 3 to 4 minutes.

2. Place the anchovies, skin-side down, into the pan and shake it so they nestle into the sauce. Cook for 3 to 4 minutes, or until the fish are cooked through and tender.

3. Drizzle loads of extra virgin olive oil over top and serve immediately with crusty bread.

Essaouira Grilled Sardines

Serves 4
10 to 12 long skewers,
soaked in cold water
if wooden

8 fresh sardines, washed and cleaned

10 ounces cherry tomatoes

4 tablespoons olive oil

1 quantity of chermoula paste (see page 183)

Lemon wedges, to serve

Sea salt

On a hot day, I drove from the dusty souks of Marrakesh, past lush orange groves, and on to Essaouira, an old seaside port city on the Atlantic coast. As the sun set over the medina, I headed to the harbor, walking past blue fishing boats bobbing in the dark water, avoiding a tangle of green nets, and on towards the rickety wooden stalls by the sea. They were lively, with the sound of the catch of the day sizzling on hot coals, and full of families gathered around little wooden tables. I ate fresh sardines, blistered from the heat of the coals, smoky and charred. Served with freshly made chermoula, tomatoes, and a local lemon that looked more Amalfi than Atlantic, this was my first bite of Moroccan seafood and I was hooked. The recipe is so easy to make and encapsulates the buzz of the harbor and bold flavors of Moroccan cooking.

1. Prepare a barbecue for high heat. Meanwhile make little slits into the sardines so that they can absorb the flavor of the sauce. Put into a mixing bowl and add 4 tablespoons of the chermoula. Season with a small pinch of salt. Toss together, making sure that the fish gets completely coated in the sauce. Cover and refrigerate for 30 minutes.

2. Skewer the fish carefully, feeding a skewer from the tail end to the head. Skewer the cherry tomatoes on a few skewers, so that they are in single rows—don't push them too tightly together. Drizzle the olive oil over the sardines and tomatoes.

3. Cook the sardines for 4 to 6 minutes each side, until cooked through and tender. Transfer to a serving dish and remove the skewers. Drizzle over some more of the chermoula.

4. Meanwhile, put the tomatoes on the barbecue and blister one side for 2 to 3 minutes. Transfer to the serving dish and remove the skewer. Serve the sardines and tomatoes immediately with lemon wedges and the remaining sauce in a bowl.

Sardine Kefta

Serves 4

FOR THE KEFTA

1 pound fresh sardine fillets, cleaned

A small handful of chopped cilantro leaves

2 teaspoons paprika

1 teaspoon ground cumin

½ teaspoon chile powder

¼ teaspoon ground black pepper

2 garlic cloves, crushed

1 tablespoon olive oil

¼ cup breadcrumbs

FOR THE SAUCE

2 long sweet green peppers (not green bell peppers)

2 tablespoons olive oil

1 carrot, cut into thin round slices

4 tomatoes, finely chopped

1 teaspoon paprika

1 teaspoon cumin

1 preserved lemon (page 184), cut in half

¼ cup pitted black olives

½ cup just-boiled water

Sea salt and freshly ground black pepper

This is a classic Moroccan seafood dish that is cooked all along the coastline, where fresh sardines are landed in abundance. The delicate fish are blended into a paste with herbs and spices and rolled into little *kefta*. These are then cooked in a rich sauce with preserved lemons and olives.

1. Put all the ingredients for the kefta into a blender. Add a pinch of salt and blend until smooth. Wet your hands to stop the fish sticking to them, then take a small piece of the mix and roll it into a ball, a little smaller than a ping-pong ball. Repeat with the rest. The mixture is quite wet, but don't worry—the *kefta* will firm up when cooking.

2. Cook the peppers on a barbecue or over a high gas flame for about 6 to 8 minutes until charred and tender. (Alternatively, roast the peppers in a 500°F oven until charred.) Put into a shallow dish and cover with plastic wrap. Leave to cool for about 5 minutes, then peel off and discard the skin and scrape out the seeds. Finely slice the flesh.

3. Heat the oil in a shallow pan over medium heat. Add the carrot slices and season with a pinch of salt. Cook for 5 to 6 minutes until soft and golden on one side. Add the *kefta*, tomatoes, peppers, paprika, cumin, preserved lemon, and olives. Pour in the just-boiled water, cover, reduce the heat to low, and cook for a further 10 minutes. Remove the lid and turn the kefta. Cook for a final 5 to 6 minutes, or until the kefta are cooked through and the sauce has thickened. Serve immediately.

Charred Squid

Serves 2

- 2 preserved lemons, seeded and finely chopped
- A handful of finely chopped cilantro leaves
- A handful of finely chopped flat-leaf parsley leaves
- 4 tablespoons olive oil
- Juice of ½ lemon
- ½ teaspoon sugar
- 14 ounces fresh squid, cleaned, with tentacles
- Sea salt and freshly ground black pepper

In the cool coastal town of Larache, the fishing port is buzzing with life. The catch of the day is displayed on wooden tables, covered in ice for restaurateurs and hungry housewives to take their pick. You can grab what you want and head to one of the nearby restaurants, who will cook your seafood over a hot grill. On my last visit, there was an abundance of fresh squid, and it inspired me to make this recipe. The smoky flavor of the charcoal grill and the sweet squid is the perfect combination, along with my mellow preserved lemon dipping sauce.

1. Mix the preserved lemons, herbs, half the oil, the lemon juice, sugar, and a good pinch of salt and pepper together in a mixing bowl. Check the balance, and add more sugar or lemon juice if required. Set aside for the flavors to develop—feel free to leave it overnight for the flavors to intensify even more.

2. Heat a griddle pan over high heat until smoking. To prepare the squid, cut the tentacles from each tube and put into a bowl. Insert a knife into the tube and cut the squid open lengthwise. Open it out into one large piece. Gently score the flesh in a criss-cross pattern, taking care not to cut right through. Add to the bowl with the tentacles. Season and pour in the remaining olive oil. Toss together.

3. Cook the tube, scored-side down, for 1 to 2 minutes, then turn and cook for a further 1 to 2 minutes until cooked through. Repeat with the remaining squid, then remove and give the tentacles the same time. Transfer to a serving plate and drizzle over the dressing. Serve immediately.

Roasted Chermoula Bream with Potatoes & Olives

Serves 4

2 sea bream, gutted and cleaned

1 quantity of chermoula paste (page 183)

10 ounces new potatoes, thinly sliced

2 tablespoons olive oil, plus extra for drizzling

14 ounces cherry tomatoes, halved

½ cup pitted black olives

1 tablespoon capers

Sea salt and freshly ground black pepper

This is such a classic Moroccan dish; fresh fish covered in chermoula, a wonderful sauce made from herbs, lemon, and paprika, and cooked with potatoes, tomatoes, and olives. I first ate this while staying with friends in Essaouira, a seaside town on the Atlantic coast. It was so delicious, cooked in the oven, and served with a little bread and a fresh arugula salad. It would make a perfect lazy lunch. To get the cooking right, make sure the potatoes are thinly sliced and remain at the bottom of the baking dish when you add the other ingredients. This way they will absorb all the cooking juices and get beautifully tender at the same time as the fish.

1. Preheat the oven to 425°F. Make a few shallow slits into the flesh of the bream and rub three-quarters of the chermoula all over them. Leave to marinate in a shallow dish for 10 to 15 minutes.

2. Drizzle a little olive oil over the base of a baking dish. Add the potatoes in a single layer and season with a pinch of salt and pepper. Top with the fish and any chermoula left in the dish. Scatter the tomatoes, olives, and capers over the top and pour over the olive oil.

3. Cut a piece of parchment paper big enough to cover the dish, and scrunch it under the cold tap. Lay it out over the fish and cover the whole dish with aluminum foil—this will help keep everything really moist in the oven. Roast for 30 to 35 minutes until the fish is cooked through and wonderfully juicy. Serve immediately with the remaining chermoula and a sprinkling of fresh flat-leaf parsley.

Seafood Bastillas

Makes 8
mini bastillas

2 salmon fillets, skin on

6 ounces peeled jumbo shrimp

1½ teaspoons ras el hanout

1 tablespoon olive oil, plus extra for greasing

1½ tablespoons butter

1½ teaspoons ground cumin

1 teaspoon paprika

3½ ounces vermicelli rice noodles, cooked, cooled, and chopped

2 small handfuls of finely chopped cilantro leaves

A small handful of finely chopped flat-leaf parsley leaves

Skin of 1 preserved lemon (see page 184), finely chopped, seeds removed

8 phyllo pastry sheets

1 free-range egg, beaten

Tomato & Garlic Sauce (page 62), to serve

Sea salt and freshly ground black pepper

The traditional *bastilla*, made with squab, was an opulent pie cooked for the sultans of Fez and it is still a specialty of the city. Today, *bastillas* have evolved to include chicken, quail, and seafood varieties. My seafood *bastillas* are delicious served with the rich tomato and garlic sauce on page 62.

1. Preheat the oven to 400°F. Line a baking sheet with foil, then grease with a little olive oil.

2. Put the salmon, skin-side down, on a plate with the shrimp. Sprinkle with a pinch of salt and 1 teaspoon of the ras el hanout.

3. Heat the oil in a non-stick frying pan over high heat. Add the salmon, flesh-side down, and sear for 1 minute. Turn and reduce the heat to medium. Cook for 2 to 3 minutes to sear the other side. Add the shrimp to the pan. Cook for a minute or so until pink on one side, then turn. Cover and remove from the heat. Set aside for 4 to 5 minutes to finish cooking.

4. Melt the butter in a small pan over medium heat. Once bubbling, remove from the heat and mix in the cumin, paprika, and remaining ras el hanout. Put the cooked noodles in a mixing bowl and pour over the butter mixture. Add the herbs, preserved lemon, and a good pinch of salt to the bowl and mix well.

5. Flake the salmon flesh, discarding the skin, and add it to the noodles with the shrimp. Mix everything together really well.

6. Take a sheet of phyllo pastry and fold down one corner to make a triangle. Cut off the excess rectangle shape and save. Fold out the triangle into a square of pastry. Cut the rectangular off-cut into two pieces. Place one piece in the center of the square. Brush the sides of the square with beaten egg.

7. Place about ½ cup of the mix into the center of the pastry. Top the mixture with the other piece of the off-cut pastry. Fold the sides tightly up and in to form a neat parcel. Flip the parcel over and place on the prepared baking sheet. Brush with beaten egg. Repeat with remaining phyllo sheets and mixture. Bake in the hot oven for 20 to 25 minutes, or until golden and crispy. Serve folded side up with the tomato and garlic sauce.

Saffron-scented Monkfish Stew

Serves 4

1 pound filleted monkfish tail, cut into 1-inch chunks

A handful of roughly chopped flat-leaf parsley leaves

A handful of roughly chopped cilantro leaves

2 garlic cloves, crushed

1 teaspoon ground cumin

1 teaspoon ground ginger

¼ teaspoon cinnamon

A pinch of saffron

4 tablespoons olive oil

1 cup couscous

3 tomatoes, finely chopped

1 tablespoon tomato purée

1 preserved lemon (page 184), seeded and finely chopped

¼ cup pitted mixed olives

2 tablespoons golden raisins

3 tablespoons sliced almonds

Sea salt and freshly ground black pepper

This decadent dish, made with monkfish, saffron, preserved lemon, and golden raisins, is a wonderful stew that's perfect served with mountains of fluffy couscous. Along Morocco's Mediterranean coast it is made with merlán, or whiting. It's a white fish with a firm texture that becomes soft and creamy when cooked. Monkfish is a wonderful substitute, and the flavor stands up to the robust Moroccan ingredients. Traditionally the couscous could be cooked above the stew to take on all the flavor, but I make a quick version separately, so that the monkfish does not overcook.

1. Put the monkfish into a mixing bowl and add the parsley, cilantro, garlic, cumin, ginger, cinnamon, and saffron. Season with salt and pepper. Pour over 2 tablespoons of the olive oil and toss everything together so that the fish is completely coated in the herbs and fragrant spices. Cover and leave to marinate for 15 minutes.

2. Meanwhile, put the couscous into a bowl. Season with salt and pepper, and pour over enough just boiled water to cover by about ¼ inch. Cover with plastic wrap and set aside for the water to be absorbed.

3. Heat a pan over medium heat and pour in the remaining oil. Add the tomatoes and tomato purée. Mix well and cook, stirring occasionally, for 5 to 6 minutes, or until the tomatoes have completely broken down. Pour over 1 cup of boiling water and mix well.

4. Put the fish and its marinade into the pan. Add the preserved lemon, olives, and raisins. Bring to a boil, cover, reduce the heat to low, and cook for 12 to 15 minutes until the fish is cooked through and tender—the flesh will have turned milky in color and be firm to the touch. Scatter over the almonds and serve immediately alongside the couscous.

Cumin-Battered Hake with Preserved Lemon Mayonnaise

Serves 4

1¼ pounds hake fillets, cut into long strips

2 teaspoons ground cumin

1 teaspoon paprika

½ teaspoon dry chermoula (page 180)

Vegetable oil, for shallow frying

1 cup semolina flour

Sea salt

TO SERVE

1 cup mayonnaise

1 preserved lemon (page 184), seeds removed, and finely chopped

Juice of ½ lemon

In souks across Morocco, fried fish is sold as a quick snack or take-out option, the classic being fried sardines dusted in a light coating of semolina flour that becomes gloriously dry and crisp once cooked. The wonderfully musty Moroccan cumin flavors the semolina and is always offered as an extra seasoning to add as you eat. Here I give a very traditional coating to hake—or merluza—and serve it with a more modern mayonnaise, flavored with preserved lemon.

1. Place the fish into a shallow dish and season both sides with cumin, paprika, chermoula, and a pinch of salt.

2. Take a wide, deep pan and add enough oil so that it will half cover the fish. Place over medium heat. Spread the semolina flour in a shallow dish. Add the fish and coat both sides. Wipe off any excess. Shallow-fry the fish for 3 to 4 minutes each side, or until cooked through and tender. Transfer to paper towels to absorb any excess oil.

3. Meanwhile, mix the mayonnaise with the preserved lemon, lemon juice, and a pinch of salt. Serve with the cooked fish.

Fouad's Paprika Shrimp

Serves 4

3 tablespoons olive oil

1 red onion, finely chopped

4 garlic cloves, roughly chopped

A handful of roughly chopped flat-leaf parsley leaves

1 teaspoon paprika

½ teaspoon ground ginger

¼ teaspoon ground black pepper

1½ cups tomato sauce

1 preserved lemon (page 184), seeds removed, and finely chopped

¼ cup hot water

1 pound peeled jumbo shrimp

Sea salt

Fresh from the azure-blue waters of the Mediterranean, these juicy shellfish were caught and cooked for my lunch by my friend Fouad, a fantastic chef who has a restaurant in Chefchaouen and a home in the tiny fishing village of Chmala, on the coast. He tossed king prawns (but you can use jumbo shrimp) in a light tomato sauce with loads of garlic, spices, and preserved lemon. The fresh style of cooking is very Mediterranean, but the flavors are distinctly Moroccan—such is the style of cooking along the northeast coast.

1. Heat the oil in a large pan over high heat. Add the onion and stir-fry for 2 to 3 minutes until soft. Add the garlic and stir-fry for 10 seconds until fragrant. Add the parsley, spices, and a good pinch of salt. Mix well.

2. Pour the tomato sauce into the pan. Add the preserved lemon and hot water. Mix well. Reduce the heat to medium and simmer, stirring occasionally, for 2 to 3 minutes until the tomato sauce thickens.

3. Add the shrimp and mix well. Cover, and cook for 4 to 5 minutes, shaking the pan occasionally, or until the shrimp are cooked through. Serve immediately.

Fried Atlantic Shrimp with Preserved Lemon & Oregano

Serves 4

4 tablespoons olive oil

4 garlic cloves, roughly chopped

1 preserved lemon (page 184), pith discarded and the skin finely chopped

1¼ pounds peeled jumbo shrimp

1 teaspoon ground cumin

½ teaspoon ground black pepper

½ teaspoon paprika

¼ teaspoon ground turmeric

¼ teaspoon chile flakes

1 teaspoon dried oregano

A handful of finely chopped cilantro leaves

A handful of finely chopped flat-leaf parsley leaves

1 lemon cut into wedges, to serve

Sea salt

These simple fried shrimp are a typical dish cooked along Morocco's Atlantic coast, where the freshly caught seafood is just incredible. The juicy shellfish cook quickly, taking on all the flavor of the garlic, preserved lemons, and herbs. When I ate this dish in the quiet beach town of Oualidia, just south of Casablanca, it was prepared with the wild oregano that grows in abundance here, and king prawns. You can make this using dried oregano, which has a similarly strong flavor, and jumbo shrimp.

1. Heat the oil in a large frying pan over medium-high heat. Add the garlic and preserved lemon and stir-fry for 10 seconds until fragrant. Add the shrimp and continue to stir-fry for 2 to 3 minutes or until just turning pink.

2. Add the spices and dried oregano to the pan, season well, and continue to stir-fry for 1 to 2 minutes until the shrimp are cooked through. Stir through the herbs and serve immediately with the lemon wedges.

Blue Lagoon Oysters

Serves 4 to 6

12 to 14 oysters, shucked, on the half shell

FOR FRESH OYSTERS
4 tablespoons red wine vinegar
Skin of 1 preserved lemon (page 184), finely chopped
3 teaspoons sugar
¼ teaspoon ground ginger
½ teaspoon paprika
A small handful of very finely chopped cilantro leaves
Crushed ice, for serving

FOR CHARGRILLED OYSTERS
3 tablespoons butter
2 tablespoons harissa (page 183)
1 lemon, quartered lengthwise

Oualidia is more than a quiet coastal town—it's the country's oyster capital. The shellfish are pulled from the crystal-clear waters of the blue lagoon that shields the town from the Atlantic. Fresh oysters are wonderful with a simple dressing sharpened with spices and lemon, but if you plan a barbecue they are also fantastic cooked on the hot coals and served with a fiery harissa butter. I've given you both options here.

IF YOU PLAN TO SERVE THE OYSTERS FRESH:

1. Put the red wine vinegar and preserved lemon in a bowl, season with salt, and add the sugar and ginger. Whisk together.

2. Place the oysters onto a tray that is covered in ice. Spoon the vinegar over the oysters so that each gets a generous amount. Put a tiny pinch of paprika over each one, and from a height, scatter over the cilantro leaves. Serve immediately.

TO SERVE CHARGRILLED:

1. Prepare a barbecue for high heat. Mix the butter and harissa together. Place in a small saucepan and heat on the barbecue until the butter melts.

2. Place the oysters on the barbecue, shells down, cover, and cook for 2 to 3 minutes. Remove the barbecue lid and drizzle a generous amount of harissa butter over each one. Cook for a further 1 to 2 minutes until bubbling. Serve immediately with lemon wedges.

Green Harissa Lobster

Serves 4

FOR THE GREEN HARISSA
A handful of flat-leaf parsley leaves
A handful of cilantro leaves
1 green chilli, seeded
1 garlic clove
1 teaspoon ground cumin
1 teaspoon ground ginger
½ teaspoon ground cinnamon
Sea salt and freshly ground black pepper

FOR THE LOBSTER
3 tablespoons butter
4 lobsters, about 1⅓ pounds each

FOR THE SALAD
2 fennel bulbs, shaved
2 baby cucumbers, shaved into long strips
2 oranges, segmented and membranes/seeds removed
Juice of 1 lemon
2 tablespoons olive oil
4 tablespoons pomegranate seeds
A handful of mint leaves

Whenever I visit a coastal town in Morocco, the first thing I do is head straight to the fish market to see what the fishermen have caught that day. You can buy fabulous seafood to cook at home, or take it to a restaurant and have them do it for you. And whenever I see lobster, I can't resist. I cook mine on the barbecue with green harissa butter. Green harissa is a spicy North African sauce made with green chiles and plenty of fresh herbs, and mixed with a little butter—it melts over the charred lobsters beautifully.

1. To make the green harissa, put all the ingredients into a blender with a really good pinch of salt and pepper. Blend into a bright green and smooth paste. Transfer to a mixing bowl and add the butter. Mash together with a fork.

2. Prepare a barbecue to cook with high heat. To prepare the lobsters, cut them in half lengthwise through the head and tail. Wash out the cavity below the head and crack the claws open. Place the lobsters, flesh-side down, on the barbecue, and sear for 2 to 3 minutes. Remove from the heat and spread each one with plenty of the harissa butter. Return to the barbecue and cook, shell-side down, for 4 to 5 minutes, or until the meat is tender. Cook the claws for about 2 minutes each side, or until you can see that the meat inside is cooked through and they are fabulously pink in color.

3. Meanwhile, make the salad. Put the fennel, cucumber, and orange segments into a mixing bowl. Add the lemon juice and olive oil, and a good pinch of salt and pepper. Toss together and transfer to a serving dish. Scatter over the pomegranate seeds and mint leaves. Serve immediately with the cooked lobsters.

Moroccan Paella

3 tablespoons olive oil,
plus extra for drizzling

2 red onions, finely chopped

4 garlic cloves, roughly
chopped

A handful of freshly chopped
cilantro leaves and stems

2 handfuls of freshly chopped
flat-leaf parsley leaves

4 tomatoes, roughly chopped

2 tablespoons tomato purée

2 teaspoons ground cumin

2 teaspoons paprika

1 teaspoon ground ginger

½ teaspoon ground turmeric

¼ teaspoon ground black
pepper

1 red pepper, halved, seeded and
cut into large pieces

8 ounces beef fillet, cut into
1-inch pieces (optional)

7 ounes monkfish, cut into
2 to 3-inch chunks

1 cup long-grain rice

1¾ cups hot fish stock

6 ounces peeled jumbo shrimp

5 ounces baby squid, washed
and cleaned

2 lemons

Harissa (page 183), to serve

Sea salt

I was working in a tiny kitchen in the heart of the beautiful blue medina of Chefchaouen, a small town high in the Rif Mountains, and my friend Fouad was preparing paella Moroccan-style, spiced with cumin, ginger, and turmeric. He cooked a fish stock with prawns, merlán— a large white fish not unlike monkfish in texture—beef, tomatoes, and spices. He poured the hot stock over a pan full of long-grain rice, which is easier to get in Morocco than traditional paella rice. He then arranged the seafood and beef from the stock over the top, and scattered squid and herbs over that. We carried the massive dish to the baker next door, who pushed the pan into his wood-fired oven to roast for 30 minutes. The finished dish was lemoned and herbed, and we tucked in. The smokiness from the oven was incredible and the flavor of the spices perfect. This was one of the most exciting dishes I have ever eaten; a marriage of cultures and an explosion of flavors.

1. Heat the oil in a large, shallow pan over medium heat. Add the onions and cook, stirring occasionally, for 3 to 4 minutes until translucent. Add the garlic, cilantro, and half the parsley. Mix well and cook, stirring occasionally, for 30 seconds until fragrant. Add the tomatoes, tomato purée, and all the spices. Add a pinch of salt and pepper, and mix well.

2. Put the peppers, beef (if using), monkfish, and rice into the pan. Mix well and pour over the hot stock. Mix once. Bring to a boil, cover, reduce the heat to low, and cook for 20 minutes, or until all the liquid has been absorbed.

3. Arrange the shrimp and squid over the top of the beautiful rice. Cover and cook for 6 to 8 minutes, or until cooked through.

4. Check the seasoning, then scatter over the rest of the parsley and squeeze over the juice of ½ lemon. Drizzle with oil and serve immediately with the rest of the lemons cut into wedges and harissa paste.

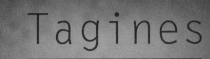
Tagines

Beef, Prune, & Egg Tagine

Serves 4

2 tablespoons olive oil

1 red onion, finely chopped

1¼ pounds beef shank on the bone, cut into 1-inch cubes

2 teaspoons ground ginger

2 teaspoons paprika

1½ teaspoons ground cumin

½ teaspoon ground black pepper

¼ teaspoon ground turmeric

A small pinch of saffron threads

½ teaspoon ground cinnamon

2 cups hot beef stock

2 tablespoons butter

10 to 12 pitted prunes

2 free-range eggs

A small handful of flat-leaf parsley leaves

Sea salt

Prepared for weddings or birthdays, this opulent tagine is rich, thick, and intense. The blend of slow-cooked meat, fragrant spices, and sweet, dried fruit is a classic Moroccan combination. The saffron lifts the dish from the everyday, giving a deep flavor and aroma to the meat. The final adornment of boiled eggs makes it even more lavish. Serve with plenty of bread to mop up all the sauce and a zesty green salad.

1. Heat the oil in a large Dutch oven over medium heat. Add the onion and cook, stirring occasionally, for 2 to 3 minutes until translucent. Add the beef and cook for 2 to 3 minutes to seal. Add the spices and a good pinch of salt. Mix well. Pour in the stock, which should just cover everything, and stir together. Bring to a boil, then cover, reduce the heat to low and cook for 1½ hours until tender. Remove the meat with a slotted spoon and place in a warm serving dish. Cover with foil and leave to rest.

2. Bring the sauce to a boil over medium heat and cook, stirring occasionally, for 30 to 40 minutes, or until rich and sticky. It will reduce by three quarters. Whisk in the butter and a pinch of salt, and then return the meat to the pan. Add the prunes and mix well. Give everything a few minutes to warm through.

3. Meanwhile, medium-boil the eggs in a pan of simmering water for about 5 to 7 minutes. Transfer to a bowl of cold water and leave to cool. Peel and cut into quarters.

4. Spoon the meat into a serving dish and pour over the sauce. Top with the eggs and flat-leaf parsley and serve immediately.

Tagines

Tagines are traditional earthenware cooking pots with a large, conical shaped lids. They are still used in many parts of Morocco today. The space created by the lid allows steam to gather, meaning meat can be cooked slowly without drying out. Visually, they are also a real show stopper when they are brought to the table. In cooking terms, a Dutch oven with a tight-fitting lid will work just as well, and some Moroccans will use a pressure cooker instead—although if you opt for this, make sure you have a beautiful serving dish in which to present your food.

Artichoke & Beef Tagine

Serves 4

2 tablespoons olive oil

4 crosscut beef shank steaks, bone removed and cut into large chunks ("crosscut" is when the shank, from the top of the leg, is cut across the bone. It's really marbled, which is why it has so much flavor, and needs a long, slow cook)

1 onion, finely chopped

2 teaspoons ground ginger

½ teaspoon ground black pepper

A large pinch of saffron threads

A small handful of roughly chopped flat-leaf parsley leaves

1¾ cups hot beef stock

A small handful of cilantro leaves and stems tied together

2 preserved lemons, quartered

8 globe artichokes, peeled and prepped, or 1 (14-ounce) can artichoke hearts, drained

¾ cup frozen peas

Sea salt and freshly ground black pepper

Artichokes grow wild in profusion in many parts of Morocco and there are two seasons—early spring and autumn—when they are at their best. This sensational dish celebrates the vegetable, braising it with slow-cooked beef shanks, plenty of black pepper, saffron, and preserved lemons. A final showering of green peas adds a fresh sweetness and vibrant pop of color. It's a wonderful, seasonal tagine from the imperial kitchens of Fez that is now cooked everywhere when the time is right. Let's not forget that artichokes, despite being utterly delicious, are quite tedious to prepare. So for my recipe, I have given you the option to use canned, which are just as delicious.

1. Heat the olive oil in a large Dutch oven over medium heat. Brown the steaks for about 3 to 4 minutes each side. Remove from the pan and set aside.

2. Add the onion to the pan and cook, stirring occasionally, for 3 to 4 minutes until a little golden. Add the spices, a good pinch of salt, and the flat-leaf parsley. Pour in the stock and mix well. Put the meat back into the pan, and add the bunch of cilantro and the preserved lemons. Cover and reduce the heat to low.

3. If using fresh artichokes, cook the meat for 1 hour, then add the artichokes to the pan and shake well so they sink into the sauce. Cover and cook for a further 1 to 1½ hours or until the meat is falling apart. If using canned artichokes, cook the meat for 2 to 2½ hours before adding them.

4. Scatter the frozen peas into the pan, increase the heat to medium, and bring to a boil. Simmer for 10 minutes to warm through and reduce the sauce a little. Cover and let sit for 10 minutes before serving to allow the meat to rest.

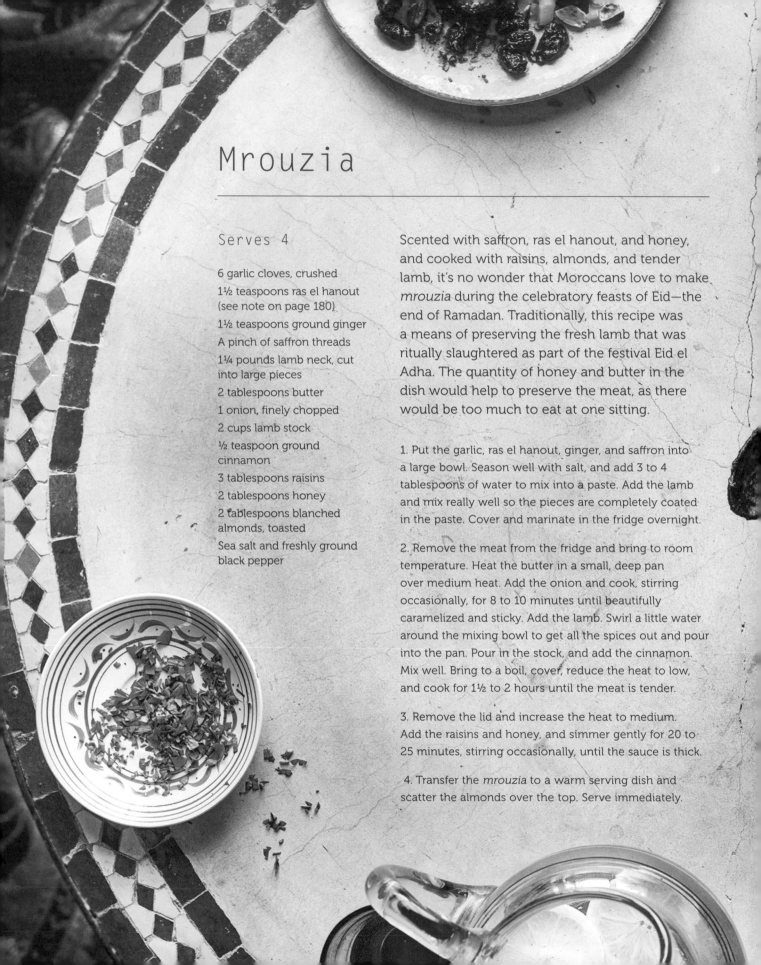

Mrouzia

Serves 4

6 garlic cloves, crushed

1½ teaspoons ras el hanout (see note on page 180)

1½ teaspoons ground ginger

A pinch of saffron threads

1¼ pounds lamb neck, cut into large pieces

2 tablespoons butter

1 onion, finely chopped

2 cups lamb stock

½ teaspoon ground cinnamon

3 tablespoons raisins

2 tablespoons honey

2 tablespoons blanched almonds, toasted

Sea salt and freshly ground black pepper

Scented with saffron, ras el hanout, and honey, and cooked with raisins, almonds, and tender lamb, it's no wonder that Moroccans love to make *mrouzia* during the celebratory feasts of Eid—the end of Ramadan. Traditionally, this recipe was a means of preserving the fresh lamb that was ritually slaughtered as part of the festival Eid el Adha. The quantity of honey and butter in the dish would help to preserve the meat, as there would be too much to eat at one sitting.

1. Put the garlic, ras el hanout, ginger, and saffron into a large bowl. Season well with salt, and add 3 to 4 tablespoons of water to mix into a paste. Add the lamb and mix really well so the pieces are completely coated in the paste. Cover and marinate in the fridge overnight.

2. Remove the meat from the fridge and bring to room temperature. Heat the butter in a small, deep pan over medium heat. Add the onion and cook, stirring occasionally, for 8 to 10 minutes until beautifully caramelized and sticky. Add the lamb. Swirl a little water around the mixing bowl to get all the spices out and pour into the pan. Pour in the stock, and add the cinnamon. Mix well. Bring to a boil, cover, reduce the heat to low, and cook for 1½ to 2 hours until the meat is tender.

3. Remove the lid and increase the heat to medium. Add the raisins and honey, and simmer gently for 20 to 25 minutes, stirring occasionally, until the sauce is thick.

4. Transfer the *mrouzia* to a warm serving dish and scatter the almonds over the top. Serve immediately.

Berber Lamb Tagine

Serves 4

14 ounces new potatoes, halved

2 tablespoons olive oil

2 red onions, finely sliced

4 garlic cloves, roughly sliced

10 ounces leg of lamb, cut into ½-inch cubes

3 zucchini, cut into ½-inch slices

2½ teaspoons paprika

2 teaspoons ground ginger

2 teaspoons ground cumin

½ teaspoon ground turmeric

¼ teaspoon ground black pepper

1¾ cups hot lamb stock

A handful of roughly chopped cilantro leaves

Sea salt

High in the Atlas Mountains, the town of Imlil lies in the shadow of the Toubkal, the highest peak in all of North Africa, at just over 13,000 feet. The little town looks like something from Middle Earth, nestled beside a river, surrounded by apple orchards. It's a very special place. I was staying with friends who, after an extremely long hike in the magnificent mountains, prepared a simple Berber tagine for me. We sat around the table to eat. The head of the family, Ahmed, dished out bread, making sure everyone had a piece. We scooped the warm, spiced vegetables out of the tagine, chatting about our day. The meat was left until last—the highlight of the meal—and again Ahmed served us to ensure we all had a share. This tagine etiquette is very traditional, with the head of the family portioning up the delicious meat at the end, so everyone can savor each mouthful and finish on a high.

1. Parboil the potatoes in lightly salted water for about 5 to 6 minutes to start them cooking. Drain and set aside.

2. Heat the oil in a large pan over medium heat and add the onions. Cook, stirring occasionally, for 4 to 5 minutes until a little golden. Add the garlic and cook for 10 seconds until fragrant.

3. Put the meat in the pan, and add the potatoes, zucchini, paprika, ginger, cumin, turmeric, and black pepper. Add a good pinch of salt and pour in the stock. Mix everything together really well and bring to a boil. Cover, reduce the heat to low, and cook for 30 minutes, or until the meat and potatoes are both soft.

4. Remove the lid and increase the heat to medium. Bubble gently for 20 to 25 minutes, until the sauce has reduced by half and is nice and thick. Check the seasoning as the potatoes soak it up. Add the cilantro and mix well. Serve immediately.

Quince & Lamb Tagine

Serves 4

2 quinces, peeled, quartered and cored

2 tablespoons olive oil

1¼ pounds lamb shoulder, off the bone and cut into 3 to 4-inch pieces

1 red onion, finely chopped

2 garlic cloves, finely chopped

1⅔ hot lamb stock

1½ teaspoons ras el hanout (see note on page 180)

1 teaspoon ground ginger

A pinch of saffron threads

¾ teaspoon ground cinnamon

The thin piece of the shoulder blade bone (optional)

3 tablespoons butter

2 teaspoons toasted sesame seeds

Sea salt and freshly ground black pepper

This lavish dish was prepared in the kitchens of the imperial cities—Fez, Meknes, Marrakesh, and Rabat—for their esteemed guests, and it still feels as decadent today. The beautiful perfume of quince as it cooks is utterly alluring, and its tartness complements the soft lamb perfectly. Including the piece of bone gives the finished dish a rich, rounded, meaty flavor.

1. Put the quinces into a pan and cover with cold water. Bring to a boil over medium heat, reduce the heat to low, and simmer for 20 to 25 minutes until tender. Drain, reserving a few tablespoons of the cooking water, and leave in the colander for a few minutes.

2. Meanwhile, heat the oil in a large, shallow pan over medium-high heat. Add the lamb and brown for 5 to 6 minutes each side until beautifully golden. Remove from the pan and set aside.

3. Reduce the heat to medium and add the onion. Cook, stirring occasionally, for 4 to 5 minutes to soften, then add the garlic and cook for 10 seconds until fragrant. Pour in the hot stock and scrape the sticky bits off the base of the pan. Add the ras el hanout, ginger, saffron, and ½ teaspoon of the cinnamon. Season well and mix together. Return the meat to the pan and add the bone, if using. Bring to a boil, cover, reduce the heat to low, and cook for about 1½ hours, or until the meat easily pulls apart with two forks. Remove the lid, and add the cooking water from the quinces. Mix well. Increase the heat to medium and bubble for 8 to 10 minutes, shaking the pan occasionally, until the sauce has reduced by over half and is really sticky. Remove the bone.

4. Meanwhile, heat half the butter in a non-stick pan over medium heat. Add the quinces, in rows, and cook for about 4 to 5 minutes until a little golden. Watch them as they suddenly color quickly. Using a pair of tongs, turn the quinces and add the remaining butter. Cook for a further 2 to 3 minutes until golden. Turn off the heat and add the remaining cinnamon, scattering it over from a height for an even finish. Turn the quinces a few times in the butter and cinnamon to ensure the slices are completely coated.

5. Transfer the quinces to the pan with the lamb. Cover and cook for 1 to 2 minutes to heat together. Scatter the sesame seeds over the top and serve immediately.

Shepherd's Chicken Tagine

Serves 4

2 tablespoons olive oil

2 pounds chicken thighs on the bone

2 red onions, finely sliced

2 teaspoons paprika

2 teaspoons ground ginger

½ teaspoon ground black pepper

1 teaspoon cumin

A pinch of saffron threads

2 handfuls of finely chopped cilantro leaves and stems

1¾ cups hot chicken stock

1 carrot, sliced into ¼-inch rounds

1 zucchini, sliced into rounds

1 eggplant, cut into 1 to 2-inch chunks

1 sweet green pepper, seeded and cut into strips

2 tomatoes, quartered

Sea salt

After a long day in the Atlas Mountains I offered to help cook dinner when we returned to the village of Tacheddirt. It was one of the moments when I realized I have been living in the city way too long. I was given a box of vegetables with a live chicken sitting on top, clucking and staring at me. Not quite what I am used to. So we got to it and prepared the chicken, which took a little longer than simply pulling back the plastic; its throat was cut in the halal manner and then plucked, cleaned, and quickly flamed to remove any little feathers. Then we got cracking on the tagine, made with local vegetables picked from the garden and wonderful wild herbs. This was simple, hearty food served with piles of bread and steaming lemon verbena tea, and we sat around the table watching the evening sky change color over the mountains.

1. Heat the oil in a large Dutch oven or tagine over medium heat. Add the chicken thighs and brown for 3 to 4 minutes each side. Remove from the pan and set aside.

2. Add the onions to the pan and cook, stirring occasionally, for 3 to 4 minutes until soft and a little golden. Add the spices, half the cilantro, and a good pinch of salt. Mix well.

3. Return the chicken to the pan and pour over the hot stock. Bring to a boil, cover, reduce the heat to low, and cook for 30 minutes.

4. Scatter the carrots into the pan and shake well so that they settle into the sauce. Add the zucchini, eggplant, pepper, and tomatoes. Cover, shake the pan well, and cook for 35 to 40 minutes, or until the chicken is cooked through and tender, and the vegetables beautifully cooked, but still with a little bite.

5. Remove the lid, increase the heat to medium-high, and cook for 8 to 10 minutes so the sauce thickens. Pour into a warm serving dish and top with the remaining cilantro. Serve immediately.

Saffron & Preserved Lemon Rabbit Tagine

Serves 4

4 tablespoons olive oil

1 rabbit, cut into 7 pieces

4 preserved lemons
(page 184)

10 garlic cloves

2 teaspoons ground cumin

2 teaspoons ground ginger

1 teaspoon ras el hanout
(see note on page 180)

1 teaspoon ground black
pepper

A pinch of saffron threads

3 bay leaves

2¾ cups hot chicken stock

A handful of finely chopped
flat-leaf parsley leaves, plus
leaves to garnish

Sea salt and freshly ground
black pepper

When in season in the northern mountains, rabbit is cooked in the villages, stewed with vegetables and wild herbs, and served with bread. And in the cities, where tagine culture is more refined, they are braised slowly with spices to accentuate the gamey flavor. My opulent rabbit tagine uses all the finest Moroccan ingredients: ras el hanout, saffron, and preserved lemons, and of course, rabbit. The meat benefits from slow and low cooking, and its gutsy flavor really stands up to the other robust ingredients.

1. Heat the oil in a large pan over medium heat and add the rabbit. Brown on all sides for about 8 to 10 minutes.

2. Meanwhile, remove the seeds from two of the preserved lemons and roughly chop the flesh and skin.

3. Add the chopped preserved lemons to the browned rabbit, along with the garlic, spices, bay leaves, and a good pinch of salt and pepper. Pour over the stock and mix everything together. It should cover the rabbit by about three quarters. Bring to a boil, cover, reduce the heat to low, and cook for 1½ to 2 hours until the meat is tender. Once the meat is cooked, transfer to a warm serving plate and cover with foil.

4. Increase the heat to medium-high and boil the cooking liquid for about 20 minutes, or until reduced down by about three-quarters, so it's nice and thick. Return the rabbit to the pan. Gently stir to coat in the sauce and heat through for a few minutes.

5. Finely slice the skin of the remaining two preserved lemons. Place the rabbit back in the serving dish, along with all the juices. Garnish with the chopped preserved lemon skin and parsley. Serve immediately.

Coastal Calamari Tagine

Serves 2

2 tablespoons olive oil

3 garlic cloves, crushed

12 ounces baby squid, cleaned

4 tomatoes, finely chopped

1 tablespoon tomato purée

1 teaspoon paprika

½ teaspoon ground cumin

A small pinch of saffron threads

2 small handfuls of finely chopped cilantro leaves

2 small handfuls of finely chopped flat-leaf parsley leaves

2 preserved lemons (see page 184)

Sea salt and freshly ground black pepper

The squid caught on the Atlantic coast of Morocco are at their best during the winter months, and local fish markets teem with them. Their flavor is really sweet and can stand up to robust herbs and spices, so they are perfect in simple tagines with cumin, paprika, and a pinch of saffron. I then use preserved lemons and herbs to make a fragrant Moroccan gremolata to scatter over the top and perfume the dish.

1. Heat the oil in a shallow pan or tagine over medium heat. Add the garlic and cook for 10 seconds until fragrant. Add the squid and cook for 2 to 3 minutes, stirring occasionally, then add the tomatoes, tomato purée, spices, and half the herbs. Season well and mix together. Cover and cook for 6 to 7 minutes, stirring occasionally, or until the tomatoes have broken down and the squid is cooked through.

2. Meanwhile, remove the pith from the preserved lemons, and finely chop the skin. Add the remaining herbs and chop together until really fine. Scatter over the cooked squid and serve immediately.

Sweet Pepper & Chile Sardine Tagine

Serves 2

3 garlic cloves, roughly chopped

A small handful of finely chopped cilantro leaves and stems

2½ teaspoons paprika

1½ teaspoons ground cumin

1 teaspoon dried oregano

3 tablespoons olive oil

1 lemon, ½ juiced and ½ sliced

8 ounces fresh sardine fillets, washed and cleaned

3 tomatoes, seeded and roughly sliced

1 sweet green pepper, seeded and roughly sliced

1 red chile, slit open down the middle

Sea salt

This is a really delicious, everyday tagine, using fresh sardines, which are caught in abundance all along the coast of Morocco. The fish are marinated in a chermoula-like mix of herbs and spices and then cooked in layers with other vegetables. If you can't find the long, thin sweet green peppers, use ordinary red bell peppers instead. They have a better flavor than the green ones, which are bitter.

1. Use a mortar and pestle to mash the garlic and cilantro with a little salt into a paste. Add 1½ teaspoons of the paprika, 1 teaspoon of the cumin, the oregano, 2 tablespoons of the olive oil, and the lemon juice, and mix well. Place in a mixing bowl. Add the sardines, mix well, cover, and leave to marinate for 30 minutes.

2. Layer the tomatoes in the base of an oiled tagine or non-stick pan. Add the pepper and scatter over the remaining paprika and cumin. Drizzle over the remaining olive oil and season with salt. Place the sardine fillets over the vegetables in an even layer. Arrange the sliced lemon over the top. Add the chile. Pour over enough water to have about ¼ inch in the base of the pan.

3. Heat over medium heat until the liquid starts to boil. Cover, reduce the heat to low, and cook for 15 to 20 minutes or until the fish are cooked and the peppers soft. Serve immediately.

Middle Atlas Trout Tagine

Serves 2

2 rainbow trout, gutted
and cleaned

2 preserved lemons

3 tablespoons olive oil

1 red onion, thinly sliced

3 cloves garlic, finely sliced

A small handful of finely
chopped flat-leaf parsley
leaves

A small handful of finely
chopped cilantro leaves

4 tomatoes, finely chopped

2 teaspoons dry chermoula
(page 180)

A pinch of saffron

¾ cup just-boiled water

3 tablespoons pitted green olives

1 tablespoon sliced almonds

Sea salt and freshly ground
black pepper

This recipe is from the town of Ifrane in the Middle Atlas. Strangely, it's also known as Little Switzerland, complete with chalets and nearby ski resort. The town also boasts one of Morocco's finest universities. In the summer, the surrounding lakes are teeming with trout. When the fish are in season, they are cooked in a number of different ways; grilled, pan-fried in butter, poached in a broth, or my favorite, cooked in a tagine. Make sure you get the freshest trout that you can to get the best flavor.

1. Slice a few slits into both sides of each fish and season with salt and pepper. Finely slice one of the preserved lemons and split between the two cavities of the fish.

2. Heat the oil in a shallow pan or tagine over medium heat. Add the onion and cook, stirring occasionally, for 5 to 6 minutes until soft. Add the garlic, flat-leaf parsley, and cilantro. Mix well and cook for 30 seconds until fragrant. Add the tomatoes then the chermoula, saffron, and a good pinch of salt and pepper. Mix well, and cook, stirring occasionally, for 4 to 5 minutes, or until the tomatoes have broken down. Pour in the just-boiled water, add the olives, and mix well.

3. Place the fish in the pan and bring to a boil. Cover, reduce the heat to low, and cook for 15 to 20 minutes, or until the fish is cooked through and tender.

4. Meanwhile, toast the almonds in a small pan, shaking occasionally, over low-medium heat until golden. Set aside to cool.

5. Serve the cooked fish with the almonds scattered over the top.

Spicy Merguez Eggs

Serves 2

2 tablespoons olive oil

1 onion, finely chopped

1 red pepper, seeded and finely chopped

1 garlic clove, finely chopped

5 ounces (4 small) merguez sausages, casings removed

1 teaspoon ground cumin

1 teaspoon paprika

2 tomatoes, finely chopped

1 tablespoon tomato purée

2 tablespoons harissa (page 183)

4 free-range eggs

½ cup Greek yogurt

A handful of finely chopped cilantro leaves

Sea salt

These fabulous baked eggs use a Moroccan sausage called merguez that is made with either lamb or beef, or a mix of the two. Packed with paprika and harissa, these long, thin orange-hued sausages impart their lovely spicy flavor to the dish as it cooks. It's the ultimate weekend brunch and a cure for anything that the night before threw at you.

1. Heat the olive oil in a large frying pan over medium heat. Add the onion and pepper and cook, stirring occasionally, for 7 to 8 minutes, or until soft and golden. Add the garlic and break in the sausages (about 5 to 6 pieces each). Mix well and cook for 1 to 2 minutes to get a little color on the sausages. You may need to add a little more oil at this stage if the pan gets too dry.

2. Mix in the cumin and paprika, then add the tomatoes, tomato purée, 1 tablespoon harissa, a good pinch of salt, and ¼ cup water. Mix everything together. Increase the heat to high and bring to a boil, stirring occasionally. Cover, reduce the heat to low, and cook for 15 minutes or until the tomatoes have broken down and the sauce is thickened. Remove the lid and cook for a further 2 to 3 minutes, stirring occasionally, until the sauce is really thick. Check the seasoning and add salt or a touch more harissa if needed.

3. Reduce the heat to medium and, using the back of a spoon, make 4 little wells in the sauce. Crack in the eggs and season with salt. Cover and cook for 4 to 5 minutes or until the egg whites have just set.

4. Meanwhile mix the yogurt with the rest of the harissa paste and a pinch of salt. To serve, scatter the cilantro over the eggs and serve immediately with the harissa yogurt.

Potato Tagine

Serves 4

2 pounds russet potatoes, peeled and halved or quartered, depending on size

4 tablespoons olive oil

1 red onion, finely sliced

2 red peppers, seeded and cut into strips

3 garlic cloves, thinly sliced

4 tomatoes, finely chopped

2 tablespoons tomato purée

1 teaspoon ground cumin

1 teaspoon ground ginger

1 teaspoon paprika

2 cups vegetable stock

1 red chile, pricked

2 teaspoons harissa (page 183)

Juice of ½ lemon

A small handful of finely chopped cilantro leaves

1 tablespoon sliced almonds

Sea salt and freshly ground black pepper

Potato tagine might not sound like much, but this delicious Moroccan meal is divine. The potatoes soak up all the spices as they cook gently in the sauce, and a drizzle of harissa oil gives a killer kick at the end. Traditionally this humble dish would be served with bread and fried fish from the souk. I enjoy it just as it is for a simple midweek supper.

1. Put the potatoes into a pan of boiling salted water and parboil for 5 to 6 minutes to cook out the rawness. Drain and set aside.

2. Meanwhile, heat half the oil in a large pan over medium heat and add the onion and peppers. Stir-fry for 3 to 4 minutes to soften. Add the garlic and mix well. Add the tomatoes, season well, and stir-fry for 2 to 3 minutes until they have broken down.

3. Add the tomato purée and spices to the pan and mix well. Pour over the stock and mix together. Add the potatoes and chile. The stock should cover the potatoes by about three quarters. Cover, reduce the heat to low, and cook for 30 to 35 minutes until the potatoes are soft, but not mushy. Remove the lid and check the seasoning—you may need more salt at this stage. Increase the heat to medium and cook for a few minutes longer to thicken the sauce so that it clings to the potatoes.

4. Meanwhile, mix the harissa with the remaining olive oil and the lemon juice.

5. Scatter the cilantro and almonds over the cooked tagine and serve immediately with the harissa oil.

Desserts

Orange Blossom & Honey Cake

Serves 10

FOR THE CAKE
1 unwaxed organic orange
2 sticks (8 tablespoons) butter, at room temperature, plus extra for greasing
1¼ cup sugar
2 tablespoons orange blossom water
6 free-range eggs
3 tablespoons vegetable oil
3 cups self-rising flour
8 ounces (2 cups) ground almonds
1½ teaspoons baking powder

FOR THE FILLING
20 ounces (about 2½ cups) ricotta cheese
10 ounces (1¼ cup) Greek yogurt
¾ cup confectioners' sugar
1 tablespoon orange blossom water

FOR THE CANDIED ORANGES
1 cup sugar
2 unwaxed organic oranges, washed and thinly sliced into rounds

FOR THE TOPPING
2 ounces honeycomb, chopped, plus some of the honey for drizzling
3 tablespoons sliced almonds
A small handful of edible rose petals

A simple orange and almond cake is a staple dessert made in homes all over Morocco. I have used those classic ingredients to make a show-stopping layer cake.

1. Preheat the oven to 350°F and grease and line three 9-inch nonstick cake pans with butter and parchment paper. Put the orange in a small pan and cover with boiling water. Boil over high heat 20 minutes until soft, then drain, chop, and blend into a purée. Set aside to cool.

2. Place the butter, sugar, and orange blossom water in a stand mixer and beat for about 5 to 6 minutes until smooth. Add the eggs, one at a time, blending each time. Pour in the oil and blend again. Sift the dry ingredients into a bowl and stir. Gradually add them to the batter, blending each time until incorporated. Add the orange purée and mix well. Divide the mixture between the prepared cake pans and bake for 25 to 30 minutes. Leave to cool.

3. Put the filling ingredients in a mixing bowl and beat together until smooth. It will be a little textured due to the grainy nature of the ricotta. Cover and chill in the fridge until needed.

4. For the candied oranges, put the sugar into a nonstick frying pan over high heat and pour in 1¾ cups water. Bring to a boil and cook for 5 to 6 minutes, shaking occasionally, until the sugar has dissolved. Add the oranges, reduce the heat to medium, and cook for 15 minutes each side, turning with tongs. Remove from the pan, shaking off any excess syrup, and lay the slices out on parchment paper to cool. Reserve the syrup.

5. Prick the tops of the cakes with a fork while they are still in the pans. Spoon the reserved syrup over them. Leave for a further 20 minutes, then remove from their pans and place on a wire rack.

6. To assemble, put one of the cakes on a cake stand, smooth over a third of the filling and top with a second cake. Add another third of the filling and top with the final cake. Smooth the remaining filling over the top of the cake, then finish with the honeycomb, candied orange slices, almonds, and rose petals. Drizzle with honey and serve with another slice of candied orange per serving.

Sfenj Doughnuts

Makes 16
little doughnuts

1 (¼-ounce) packet active dry yeast

4 tablespoons plus 1 teaspoon superfine sugar

3½ cups all-purpose flour, plus extra for dusting

A pinch of salt

1 free-range egg, whisked

½ stick (4 tablespoons) butter, melted

Vegetable oil for frying, about 1 cup

1 teaspoon cinnamon

3 to 4 tablespoons honey

Salt

From my seat on the terrace at my friend Muhammad's house in the tiny village of Hommar, watching the rising sun's rays slowly creep over the Rif Mountains and into the valley was spectacular. I was mesmerized. Well, until he appeared with a plate of doughnuts and some coffee for my breakfast—that distracted me! This dish, called *sfenj*, is made with an unsweetened dough, cooked, then covered in sugar and typically served as breakfast. I have slightly adapted my recipe in favor of a lighter dough, and I drizzle them with honey, which ensures the sugar and cinnamon coating sticks to the surface.

1. Put the yeast into a measuring cup and pour in scant 1½ cups warm water. Add 1 teaspoon sugar, mix well, and leave for 5 minutes, until bubbling.

2. Mix the flour with a pinch of salt. Add the egg and butter and begin to bring together to form a dough. Slowly add the yeast mixture, a little at a time, mixing together until you have a light, slightly sticky dough. You might not need all the liquid. Turn onto a floured surface and knead until smooth. Place in an oiled mixing bowl, cover, and leave for 1 hour to rise. Divide into 16 even balls.

3. Heat the vegetable oil in a deep-sided pan over medium-high heat. You will need to adjust the heat as you go so it does not get too hot and burn the dough. To check the temperature, drop in a small piece of dough. It should bubble nicely and turn a light golden brown after 20 to 30 seconds.

4. Take one of the dough balls and roll into a sausage shape. Wrap it round the four fingers of one hand and seal to form a circle. Carefully place it into the hot oil and fry for 45 seconds to 1 minute each side, or until puffed up and golden. Use a slotted spoon to lift it onto paper towels to drain the excess oil and keep covered on a warm serving dish. Repeat with the rest of the dough.

5. Mix together the sugar and cinnamon in a small shallow dish. Drizzle the cooked doughnuts with honey and dunk into the sugar mix to coat the tops. Return to the serving dish and serve immediately.

Mini M'hencha

Makes 6

2 cups blanched almonds

2 sticks (½ pound) butter at room temperature

¼ fresh nutmeg, grated

3½ teaspoons ground cinnamon

4 tablespoons orange blossom water

5 tablespoons honey

3 tablespoons sugar

6 sheets phyllo pastry

2 tablespoons flour mixed with a little water to form a paste

1½ tablespoons melted butter

FOR THE GLAZE

2 teaspoons orange blossom water

6 tablespoons honey

A decadent dessert that is made for celebrations, *M'hencha* or "snake cake" is a fabulous coil of phyllo pastry that is stuffed with almonds, baked until crisp, and then drenched in honey. Traditionally this would be made as one large pastry to cut into wedges for a dessert. However, in the sophisticated coffee shops of the cities, little *m'hencha* are served as a snack to enjoy with thick Arabic coffee. The pastries are deep-fried until crisp and then dunked in a mixture of honey and orange blossom water.

1. Preheat the oven to 400°F.

2. Put the almonds in a food processor and blend until finely ground. Add the butter, nutmeg, cinnamon, orange blossom water, honey, and sugar to form a thick paste.

3. Place a sheet of pastry on a clean board. Take about a sixth of the nut mix and roll it into a long, thin sausage shape and place it on the pastry, near the bottom edge. You want it to extend the length of the pastry, allowing a little space at the sides. Brush the edges with the flour and water mix. Roll the pastry over the nut paste to form a cigar shape. Then starting at one end, roll the cigar into a spiral to resemble a coiled snake. Brush the end of the spiral with more flour and water paste and tuck the exposed piece under and inside another fold of pastry to secure. Place onto a lined baking sheet. Repeat with the remaining pastry sheets.

4. Brush the tops of the *m'hencha* with the melted butter and bake for around 20 minutes, or until golden and crisp.

5. Meanwhile, make the glaze. Mix together the honey and orange blossom water in a small bowl. Drizzle all over the baked *m'hencha*. Leave to cool, then serve immediately.

Ghoriba

Makes 8 cookies

1⅓ cups whole almonds, unskinned
¾ cup confectioners' sugar
¼ teaspoon baking powder
1 free-range egg, separated
¼ cup sliced almonds
A tiny pinch of sea salt

In the heart of the Essaouira's medina, Pâtisserie Boujemaa has been making exquisite cookies and pastries for years. It's a take-out bakery and opens late, so you can get your on-the-go sugar fix whenever you need it. Their *ghoriba*—almond cookies—are the best. You find different varieties all over Morocco, but theirs are real winners; super chewy, a little like a macaron, and intensely nutty. This is my version. To get the best texture, cool for 4 to 5 minutes on a wire rack, and then put them in the fridge. The temperature almost shocks them, so they firm up quicker and go even chewier.

1. Preheat the oven to 400°F and line a baking sheet with parchment paper. Spread out the almonds on a separate baking sheet and roast for 6 minutes. Remove from the oven and leave to cool. Once cool, put into a food processor and blend until fine. This will take a couple of minutes. Add the confectioners' sugar and baking powder and blitz together. Pour in the egg yolk and mix together. Scrape the mix into a bowl and set aside.

2. Meanwhile, add the salt to the egg white and whisk until soft peaks form. Add to the almond mixture and mix together to form a nice sticky dough. Divide the dough into 8 balls. If the dough is sticking to your hands, rinse them; a little water stops the dough from sticking. Gently flatten each one with the palm of your hands and place, spaced well apart, on the lined baking sheet. Push a few sliced almonds into the top of each cookie, then bake in the oven for 10 to 12 minutes, or until risen and the cookie edges and sliced almonds are a little golden.

3. Remove from the oven and leave to cool for a few minutes. Transfer to a plate and cool completely in the fridge. Serve immediately with a strong espresso.

Pomegranate & Rosewater Mille-feuille

During the day, as you wander the maze of little streets that make up the medina of Marrakesh, you will wind up in Jemaa El Fna Square, and when you do, you'll need a coffee and a pastry. Head round the back of Café France to Al Jawda, in the Rue de la Liberté. It's a sophisticated pâtisserie, filled with a fabulous array of sweet treats: coconut cookies, macarons, date-filled *makroots*, and stunning mille-feuille. Moroccans love mille-feuille, the classic French pastry stack spread with custard. It's one of the many hangovers from the French Protectorate in Morocco. Today, café culture is rife and families enjoy tucking into tea and mille-feuille for afternoon gossip on the weekend. My version is slightly more modern, flavored with pomegranate and rosewater, and made with a mascarpone cream instead of the custard. This really is a stunning centerpiece for an afternoon tea, or swanky dinner party.

1. Preheat the oven to 400°F and line a baking sheet with parchment paper. Roll out the pastry into a large rectangle about 12 by 14 inches in size. Place on the lined baking sheet and prick all over with a fork. Cover the pastry with more parchment paper and top with another baking sheet—this will stop the pastry from rising. Bake for 20 to 25 minutes until golden. Remove from the oven and transfer to a wire rack to cool.

Serves 6 to 8

11 ounces storebought puff
pastry (about 1½ sheets)
2⅓ cups heavy cream
8 ounces mascarpone cheese
1¼ cups confectioners' sugar
2 teaspoons rosewater
½ cup pomegranate seeds
1½ tablespoons dried rose
petals, to decorate

2. Meanwhile, whisk the cream until soft peaks form. Add
the mascarpone, ½ cup of the confectioners' sugar, and the
rosewater. Fold together until smooth. Cover and refrigerate.

3. Divide the remaining confectioners' sugar between two bowls.
Mix one with 1 tablespoon of water and stir into a thick, white
paste. Now muddle 2½ tablespoons of the pomegranate seeds
and drain off the juice. There should be just over a tablespoon.
Mix this into the second bowl of confectioners' sugar to form a
slightly thinner pink icing.

4. Cut the cooled pastry into three even rectangles. Place one of
them onto a serving board and spread half of the cream mixture
over the top. Flatten and even out with a knife. Top with another
piece of pastry and smooth over the remaining cream mixture.
You can run a knife around the sides and smooth out the cream,
so that you have nice sharp edges if you like.

5. Spread the white icing over the top of the third piece of pastry.
Place on the mille-feuille. Using a teaspoon, drizzle the pink icing
over the top. Run a cocktail stick around to swirl it and mess it up
so you have your very own Jackson Pollock.

6. Scatter over the pomegranate seeds and rose petals. Leave to
set for a few minutes, then serve immediately.

Rosewater & Lemon Ricotta Cheesecake

Serves 10

FOR THE CHEESECAKE
7 tablespoons butter, plus extra for greasing
10 ounces (about 5) graham crackers
1 pound cream cheese
1½ cups ricotta cheese
1 cup confectioners' sugar
1 tablespoon cornstarch
2 tablespoons rosewater
Zest and juice of 1 lemon
4 free-range eggs

FOR THE TOPPING
1¼ cups heavy cream
2 tablespoons confectioners' sugar
1 teaspoon rosewater
Zest and juice of 1 lemon
4 figs, quartered
1 orange, peeled, segmented, and chopped, membrane removed
½ cup pomegranate seeds
Honey, to drizzle

While staying at the rather fabulous Riad Fes, a stunning converted palace in the medina in Fes el Bali, the chefs showed me several very modern desserts, including a cheesecake flavored with rosewater, and served with citrus fruits. I loved the idea of combining classic Moroccan fruits and flavors with a European-style cheesecake. Here I have gone for a baked cream cheese and ricotta base and a pillowy soft layer of cream, lightly perfumed with lemon and rosewater, and topped with figs, orange, and pomegranate.

1. Preheat the oven to 350°F and grease and line a 9-inch springform cake pan with butter and parchment paper.

2. Melt the butter in a small pan over medium heat. Crumble the crackers into a food processor and blend until fine. Transfer to a mixing bowl and add the melted butter. Mix together and scrape out into the lined cake pan. Press the crumbs firmly into the base to form a really well-packed layer. Refrigerate for 1 hour.

3. Put the cream cheese and ricotta into a blender and blend until smooth. Add the confectioners' sugar and cornstarch , and blend together for 30 seconds. Add the rosewater, lemon juice and zest, then the eggs, one at a time, and blend until smooth—check there are no lumps. Pour into the cake pan and bake for 1 to 1¼ hours, or until just set with a golden tinge at the edges. Allow to cool in the pan, then refrigerate for a few hours.

4. When you are ready to serve, pour the cream into a mixing bowl and add the confectioners' sugar, rosewater, and lemon zest and juice. Whisk until soft peaks form.

5. Remove the cheesecake from the pan and put on a cake stand. Spoon the cream on top. Arrange the figs and orange segments and scatter over the pomegranate seeds. Finally, drizzle with honey so it oozes down the sides, and serve immediately.

Pomegranate & Chocolate Cake

Serves 8 to 10

FOR THE CAKE
1 cup self-rising flour
1 teaspoon baking powder
½ cup plus 2 tablespoons cocoa powder
¾ cup light brown sugar
3 free-range eggs
2 sticks (½ pound) butter, melted, plus extra for greasing
2 tablespoons pomegranate molasses
2 tablespoons honey
1¼ cups Greek yogurt
Sea salt

FOR THE TOPPING
⅔ cup heavy cream
3½ ounces dark chocolate
1 tablespoon honey
A handful of pomegranate seeds

If you visit Morocco in autumn you will notice fresh pomegranates wherever you go. The beautiful seeds of these fruits are eaten after a meal, squeezed for a refreshing drink, or scattered, jewel like, over sweet and savory dishes. This fantastic sticky cake uses tangy-sweet pomegranate molasses in the base, and the vibrant ruby-red seeds are scattered over the top to add a pop of color and refreshing bite when you eat the cake.

1. Preheat the oven to 350°F and grease and line a 9-inch springform cake pan with butter and parchment paper. Sift the flour into a mixing bowl. Add the baking powder, cocoa powder, sugar, and a pinch of salt. Mix together gently to combine the ingredients.

2. Beat the eggs until really fluffy and light in color using a hand-held mixer.

3. Pour the melted butter and pomegranate molasses into the flour and mix together. Fold in the honey and yogurt, and then add the beaten eggs, a little at a time, and fold together until completely combined.

4. Scrape the mix into the cake pan and roughly smooth over. Bake for around 25 to 30 minutes or until risen and the sides are just pulling away from the pan. The cake will still be a bit wobbly, but it will firm up as it cools. Remove from the oven and set aside to cool in the pan.

5. Meanwhile, heat the cream in a pan over low heat. Break the chocolate into a small mixing bowl and add the honey. Pour the hot cream over the chocolate and gently stir together until velvety smooth. Leave for 10 minutes to cool and thicken.

6. Spoon the topping over the cake and spread out using the back of a spoon so that it drizzles down the sides. Scatter the pomegranate seeds over the top and leave to set before serving.

Fragrant Figs & Orange

Serves 2

2 oranges
6 cloves
6 cardamom pods
2-inch stick of cinnamon
4 tablespoons sugar
10 dried figs
A small handful of
mint leaves

Threaded onto string and hanging from bustling market stalls, dried figs can be found all over Morocco. They are eaten as a snack, and used to welcome new guests into the home. The fruits are also cooked with meat or made into fragrant desserts. This simple technique of poaching the dried figs in sugar syrup, with an array of spices, makes such a easy dessert.

1. Peel 2 large strips from one orange, then peel and cut both into segments.

2. Put 1 cup of water into a small pan. Put the strips of orange peel into the water and add the cloves, cardamom, cinnamon stick, and sugar. Bring to a boil over high heat, and cook for 4 to 5 minutes until the sugar dissolves.

3. Meanwhile, soak the figs in cold water for 5 minutes. Drain and add to the sugar syrup. Bring back to a boil. Reduce the heat to low and simmer gently for 20 to 25 minutes, or until the figs have swollen and the sauce has reduced down. Transfer to a serving bowl and leave to cool. Add the orange segments and top with the mint. Serve immediately.

Halwat Tmar

Makes around 20 pastries

1 pound Medjool dates

3 tablespoons blanched almonds

2 tablespoons sliced pistachios

½ teaspoon orange blossom water

½ teaspoon ground cinnamon, plus a pinch for decoration

10 oz readymade pie dough (about 2 pie shells)

1 free-range egg, whisked

At the end of the summer in the lush green oasis that surrounds the town of Skoura in the Draâ Valley, the date palms are swollen with their orange fruits. This valley is the date basket of Morocco, where torrid summer temperatures and water from the Draâ River provide the perfect growing conditions for date palms. Dates are one of the oldest cultivated fruits in the world and formed a staple part of the diet and wealth (since dried dates could be stored and exported easily) of desert communities throughout North Africa and the Middle East. Dates are mentioned more than any other fruit in the Koran, and it is advised to break the fast during Ramadan with a date. The dried dates are used to flavor tagines, stuffed with walnuts for a snack, and used as a filling for various desserts. These perfect pastries are made using soft Medjool dates and bright green pistachio nuts scented with orange blossom. They make a wonderful sweet treat with a cup of fresh mint tea.

1. Preheat the oven to 400°F and line a baking sheet with parchment paper. Put the dates into a bowl. Barely cover with hot water, and leave to soak for 10 minutes. Drain. Peel off any skin that comes away easily, but don't worry if you can't remove all of it. Pick out the pits and set the dates aside.

2. Put the nuts into a food processor and blend to a fine rubble. Add the dates to the food processor with the orange blossom water and cinnamon. Blend until completely mixed.

3. Roll out the pastry into a large rectangle about 10 by 17 inches in size and prick all over with a fork. Cut in half. Wet your hands and place a long line of the filling down the center of each rectangle. Roll the pastry up and over the filling like a cigar. Cut each one into 1-inch pieces. Place on the lined baking sheet and brush with the beaten egg. Bake for 15 to 20 minutes or until nicely golden. Leave to cool and serve immediately.

Good Morning Marrakesh Orange & Dates

Serves 4

½ cup Medjool dates

1 tablespoon honey

1 tablespoon orange blossom water

4 oranges, segmented, membrane removed from each segment

TO SERVE

Greek yogurt

3 tablespoons roasted sliced almonds

A small handful of roughly chopped mint leaves

Grown all over the country, oranges are eaten in abundance, and this classic combination of tangy citrus fruit and sweet dates is a perfect yogurt topper for breakfast. The dates mellow in the honey and take on the fragrance of the orange blossom water, which works in beautiful contrast to the sweet-sour orange pieces. You can also serve this as wonderful after-dinner palate cleanse.

1. Pit and finely slice the dates. Put them in a mixing bowl and add the honey and orange blossom water. Mix well, cover with plastic wrap, and leave for 1 hour.

2. Add the orange segments to the dates and toss together. Divide between four bowls, fill with yogurt, and scatter over the sliced almonds and mint leaves.

Essentials

Mint Tea

Prepared with Chinese green tea, sugar, and fresh mint, mint tea is the welcome drink of Morocco. Traditionally, everything is put into a metal teapot and left to brew for a few minutes. Then a glass is poured, with the teapot raised up into the air and away from the glass while pouring, creating an impressive-looking stream of tea. This helps the liquid to cool. The glass of tea is then poured back into the teapot, and this process is repeated several times to help the flavors develop. The tea is then poured into glasses filled with more fresh mint. Sugar is used to bring out the flavor, and you can really taste the difference. It also helps to tone down the bitterness of the green tea. I don't have much of a sweet tooth, so often leave it out altogether, or add just a pinch to help magnify the mint.

Cumin Salt

Makes about ½ cup

4 tablespoons cumin seeds
2½ tablespoons sea salt

Moroccan cumin is some of the best in the world. The spice is also used as a seasoning, sprinkled over salads, grilled meats, and soups. It is often served at the table, with salt, so that you can add more as you like.

1. Heat a small frying pan over medium heat. Add the cumin seeds and reduce the heat to low. Toast the seeds, shaking the pan occasionally, for 3 to 3½ minutes, or until the aroma is really strong. Transfer the seeds to a plate and leave to cool.

2. Grind the cumin seeds to a fine powder. Turn into a small dish, add the salt and mix well. This brilliant blend will last for about 6 to 8 weeks; just store in an airtight container and use when you like.

Dry Chermoula

Makes about ¼ cup

2 tablespoons ground cumin
1 tablespoon ground coriander
2 teaspoons chile powder
2 teaspoons paprika
1 teaspoon ground cinnamon
1 teaspoon allspice
1 teaspoon ground ginger
½ teaspoon ground turmeric

Perfect for seafood, this dry chermoula is a simple blend of spices that can be used to flavor grills and tagines. It's generously sprinkled on before cooking, to impart its fragrant notes, and then, once cooked, added as an extra seasoning.

Mix all the ingredients together in a dish. This will keep for 6 to 8 weeks in an airtight jar.

Ras el Hanout

Made with 30 to 40 different spices, herbs, and petals, *ras el hanout* means "top of the shop," as spice merchants would take a pinch from the top of the jars of their freshest spices and mix them together. There are many variations, but all contain cardamom, cloves, coriander, cumin, ginger, mace, nutmeg, rose petals, cinnamon, and black pepper. This opulent blend adds flavor, color, and aroma. Normally I advocate trying to make something at home. But in this case, do as the Moroccans do and buy *ras el hanout* already ground.

Chermoula Paste

Makes about 1¼ cups

4 garlic cloves, roughly chopped

1 large bunch cilantro leaves and stems

1 large handful of flat-leaf parsley leaves

2 teaspoons ground cumin

3 teaspoons smoked paprika

1 teaspoon sugar

Juice of 1 lemon

½ cup olive oil

Pinch of sea salt

Originating in North Africa, this punchy paste is a mix of herbs, spices, garlic, lemon, and olive oil. The flavors work beautifully with grilled or baked fish and a little dollop can freshen up tagines and soups. I also love it with barbecued chicken and grilled steaks—the tartness cuts through fatty meat like lamb beautifully.

Put everything into a food processor with ½ cup water and blitz together until smooth. Check the seasoning and if perfect, transfer to a serving bowl or jar. Cover and leave for at least an hour in the fridge for the flavors to develop. I love to leave this overnight, as the flavor is even better the next day. This will keep for 6 to 8 weeks in the fridge in an airtight container.

Harissa

Makes about 1¼ cups

5 dried chiles

1 teaspoon caraway seeds

1 teaspoon cumin seeds

5 fresh red chiles

2 garlic cloves

2 tablespoons olive oil

Juice of ½ lemon

½ teaspoon rosewater

Sea salt

Harissa is often served as a condiment on the side of a tagine, or with classic cold salads to add heat. Traditionally it's made with baklouti peppers. I find that a mix of fresh red chiles roasted and ground with dried red chiles gives a great smoky flavor and just the right heat.

1. Heat a non-stick pan over medium heat. Add the dried chiles and toast them, shaking the pan occasionally, for 3 to 4 minutes. Remove from the pan and set aside. Add the caraway and cumin seeds, and dry fry them for 2 to 3 minutes, shaking the pan regularly. Turn onto a plate to cool, then grind to a fine powder.

2. Meanwhile, prick the fresh chiles with a sharp knife and char them over a high flame or under the broiler for 4 to 6 minutes, turning. Let cool, peel, remove the tops, and scrape out the seeds.

3. Soak the dried chiles in a bowl of warm water for about 20 to 25 minutes to soften. Drain well. Cool, peel off the skin, then remove the tops and scrape out the seeds. Put the flesh into a mini blender and add the remaining ingredients. Add the roasted chiles and blitz into a smooth paste. Scrape into a serving dish and use as required. This will keep for about 2 weeks in the fridge.

Preserved Lemons

Makes 1 quart jar

5 unwaxed lemons
6 tablespoons sea salt
1 teaspoon nigella seeds
1 teaspoon coriander seeds
2 bay leaves
Juice of 4 to 6 lemons

One of the key flavors in Moroccan cooking, preserved lemons have been used in Arabic recipes since the 11th and 12th centuries. The fruit is pickled to last the winter. But the alchemy that happens is amazing. The fermenting mellows the flavor of the fruit—the rind becoming soft and sweet, and the pith slightly more intense and sharp. Signature Moroccan dishes—like chicken with preserved lemons and olives or lamb tangia—rely on the fragrance of this ingredient, but it's also fantastic to add a background note to tagines and salads, or it can be mixed into mayonnaise or yogurt for a quick dipping sauce, and served as an alternative to a lemon slice in a martini. The pickling juice is also perfect to use in salad dressings, as it takes on all the flavor notes of the fruits and spices.

1. Cut a cross shape through the lemons lengthwise right down the middle, as if cutting them into quarters, but still intact. Rub salt all over the inside of the lemons, and really pack it in.

2. Put the nigella seeds, coriander seeds, and bay leaves in a 1-quart sterilized jar. Push the lemons into the jar, adding any of the leftover salt. Top up the jar with the lemon juice so that the lemons are completely covered. You might find it helps to push in one of the squeezed-out lemon halves, from the juicing, to help keep the salted lemons submerged in the jar.

3. Leave them to ferment for at least a month, shaking the jar a couple of times. The longer you leave them, the more the flavor develops.

4. To use, rinse the salt off the lemons and remove the seeds. The zest is the most fragrant part—just slice or finely chop. When you need more flavor, the pith is also delicious. Finely chop it into a pulp and add to whatever you are preparing. These will keep for months as long as they are submerged.

Steamed Couscous

1 pound couscous
6 tablespoons olive oil

Couscous is one of the most loved dishes in Morocco. It's a celebration, always cooked in abundance to feed a crowd, perfect for the meal on Friday, the holy day, when the whole family gathers together to eat. The couscous is steamed two or three times to separate the grains and washed in between cooking so the grains stay fluffy and light. The grains are cooked in a couscoussier, a large pot that is used to cook a meat or vegetable stew, with a steamer for the couscous above. The purpose is for the couscous to take on the flavor of the stew, and the two- to three-stage cooking process keeps the grains dry, so that they absorb more of the cooking sauce when the stew is served. You can really see and taste the difference compared with simply soaking couscous in boiling water. The couscous is plated up on a huge dish, a well made in the center to hold the stew, and some of the cooking liquor spooned over the top to add more flavor. This is placed in the middle of the table for everyone to enjoy.

1. Heat a steamer over medium-high heat, with enough water to last for about an hour. Spread the couscous in a large dish. Add half the oil and pour over ¼ cup of cold water. Massage the couscous so that the grains are coated in the oil. Scrape the couscous into the steamer and steam for 30 minutes.

2. Return the couscous to the dish, and add ¼ cup of cold water and a good pinch of salt. Mix well to help separate the grains. Then add the remaining oil and mix again. Return to the steamer, and steam for 30 to 40 minutes until beautifully fluffy and soft. Fluff with a fork and serve immediately in a warm serving dish.

Fig & Lavender Jam

**Makes about 2
half-pint jars**

2 pounds fresh figs, each cut
into 8 pieces, stems removed
2 cups superfine sugar
½ teaspoon lavender flowers
Juice of 2 lemons

High in the Rif Mountains of Morocco, figs grow in abundance. During the summer the trees, swollen with fruits, are harvested. The figs are eaten fresh or dried in the hot summer sun to last through the winter. The glut of fresh fruit is also used to make jam, which will last for months, bringing a ray of sunshine into cold kitchens later in the year. This lavender-perfumed fig jam is so easy to make and the flavor is wonderful. The jam will keep in sterilized jars for up to 6 months.

1. Put the figs into a large pan and pour over the sugar. Add the lavender flowers, lemon juice, and 1 cup water, and place over medium heat. Cook, stirring occasionally, for 15 to 20 minutes, until the sugar has dissolved and the figs have broken down. Mix well.

2. Reduce the heat to low, cover, and cook for 1 to 2 hours, stirring every 20 minutes and skimming off any scum, until very thick. It should set naturally on a chilled saucer —look for little lines when you push it with your forefinger.

3. Transfer to two sterilized jam jars and leave to cool. Serve with fresh bread and butter.

Index

Acknowledgments

To make a book like this, there are so many people involved, all of whom I want to thank. In Morocco, Alan and Jo Keohane—I couldn't have done it without you. Thanks guys, it was a blast! Heather and Abdel Benhrima, who plied me with rosé at Villa Dinari; Naima and Hasna, the best local cooks I know; Beatriz Maximo, who opened up her fabulous desert home; my fixers, Lachen and Touria; Michele and Gail at Plan It Morocco; Mandy Sinclair at Tasting Marrakesh; and Faycal Alaoui at Visit Morocco.

The book has had the best team working on it, so it's with huge claps and cheers that I thank everyone at Kyle Books—Kyle, thanks for pep talks over a calming glass of red and Judith for commissioning another book. My editor, Tara, for being the best damn editor ever (fact!), and making me look like the most polished writer in the biz. And any minute now, Carmen, and the rest of the publicity team for working their magic. Thanks also to Dr. Lise Storm of the University of Exeter for her expert knowledge.

My fabulous production "dream team"—you rock! Martin Poole, food photographer extraordinaire; Rosie Reynolds, dream food stylist and all-round babe; Wei Tang, prop maestro; Patrick Budge, my art director; and Alan Keohane, who did the stunning travel photography.

And, of course, my family. All the Gregory-Smiths and Orringes. I bloody love you lot!

An Hachette UK Company
www.hachette.co.uk

First published in Great Britain in 2017 by
Kyle Books, an imprint of Kyle Cathie Ltd
Carmelite House
50 Victoria Embankment
London EC4Y 0DZ
www.kylebooks.co.uk

This edition published 2018

ISBN 978 1 90948 790 1

Text © 2017 John Gregory-Smith
Design © 2017 Kyle Books
Food photographs © 2017 Martin Poole
Location photographs © 2017 Alan Keohane
Map on endpapers © 2017 Neil Gower

Distributed in the US by Hachette Book Group,
1290 Avenue of the Americas, 4th and 5th Floors,
New York, NY 10104

Distributed in Canada by Canadian Manda Group,
664 Annette St., Toronto, Ontario, Canada M6S 2C8

Project Editor: Tara O'Sullivan
Editorial Assistant: Isabel Gonzalez-Prendergast
Copy Editor: Stephanie Evans
Designer: Patrick Budge
Food photographer: Martin Poole
Location photographer: Alan Keohane
Food Stylist: Rosie Reynolds
Prop Stylist: Wei Tang
Editorial Adaptation, US: Christopher Steighner
Production: Nic Jones and Gemma John

Printed and bound in China

10 9 8 7 6 5 4 3 2 1